Nehemiah
BUILD
THAT WALL

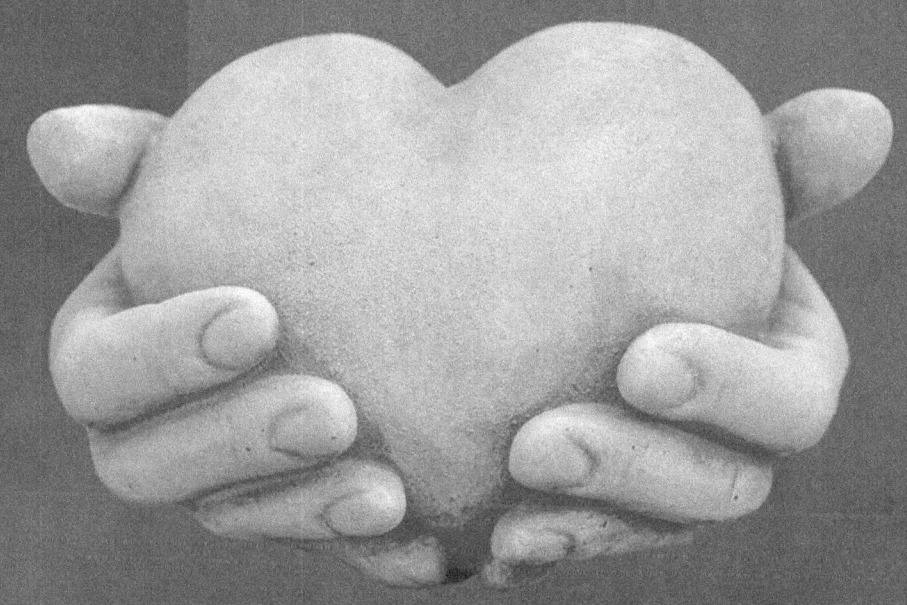

8-SESSION BIBLE STUDY

JACQUIE HOEKSTRA

BUILD
THAT WALL

JACQUIE HOEKSTRA

Second Edition
GLORY PEAK PUBLISHING

 **GLORY PEAK PUBLISHING**

Brownsville, Oregon
jacquiehoekstra.com

ISBN: 979-8-9909035-1-7

Unless otherwise noted, all Scripture quotations are from The Holy Bible, New King James Version, © 1982, Thomas Nelson, Inc. Scriptures taken from GOD'S WORD®. © 1995, 2003, 2013, 2014, 2019, 2020 by God's Word to the Nations Mission Society. Used by permission.

All references listed in the endnotes are used by permission. Editing services provided by Amanda Bird of The Book Nest

Cover photo used by permission from Alexa from Pixabay, https://pixabay.com/users/alexas_fotos-686414)

Revision 1/29/2025

Contents

Foreword

The Book of Nehemiah has long been a source of great encouragement to the Body of Christ. Nehemiah reminds us of the impact that one individual can have in their community and nation simply by following God, especially during seasons of difficulty. Even though Nehemiah's journey happened during the 5th Century BC while serving as a cup-bearer to King Artaxerxes of Persia, how he navigated his context is not very different from how we are called to navigate our context within the 21st Century. Hebrews states "Jesus Christ *is* the same yesterday, today, and forever" (Hebrews 13:8). God has not changed in how He leads His people, regardless of whether they are a man or woman, young or old, new believer or seasoned sage. Whether one works in the marketplace, stays home to care for their family, has small children, or has never been married, the God of the Universe works through His sons and daughters in every context.

God is not the only one who has not changed. The enemy also stays true to his nature. In the book of John, Jesus states, "The thief does not come except to steal, and to kill, and to destroy. I have come that they may have life, and that they may have *it* more abundantly" (John 10:10). Jesus reminds us of the schemes of the enemy to steal, kill and destroy, while also reminding us of His plans and purposes to release His abundant life. From the beginning of humanity's time on earth to now, the goal of the enemy has been to lie and steal. We see it in the lives of Adam and Eve, the life of Nehemiah, and our own personal lives.

Jacquie Hoekstra understands not only the faithfulness of God but also the consistency of the enemy. Through this study, she shares the impact God has had through the book of Nehemiah in her own personal journey. Where the enemy was up to his old tricks in Jacquie's life, her surrender to Jesus in that season led her to not only recognize the enemy's tactics but also to know how to stand on the truth of who God is and who she is in God. Jacquie has a love for the Word of God, with a passion to dig in deep. Her studies demonstrate that desire, and give place for the Bible study participant to dig in deep as well. She invites the reader to travel with Nehemiah to see what he came up against in his life, and how he responded to his context. As we travel with Nehemiah, Jacquie also invites the reader to take those things they come up against in their own lives and invite the Lord to speak to them through the pages of Nehemiah's life.

As you say yes to this journey, I pray that the Word of God will come alive to you in ways you have never experienced before. As you look at Nehemiah's life, I pray you will grasp in a greater way who God is and who He has called you to be as His son or daughter. I trust that as the Lord's light shines on the schemes of the enemy in Nehemiah's life, the Lord will highlight areas where the enemy's schemes have affected you in your own life. And as the Lord reveals the enemy's tactics, and provides His truth, you will walk in a greater freedom that will change your life. Then, your changed life will affect how you interact with your family, friends, and community.

Nehemiah said yes to God in rebuilding the wall. His yes not only partnered with God's plans for Israel but also transformed Nehemiah's life. It is as we say yes to what Jesus is inviting us into—His plans and purposes—that we see the greatest transformation in our own lives...so blessings to your YES in Him!

Nicole Cade
Senior Pastor
Valley Christian Center
Albany, Oregon

Introduction

Several years ago, I went through a challenging season, and Nehemiah gave me tools to recognize and overcome the enemy's tactics. I was so moved by the experience I wrote several blogs to help others do the same. I soon realized the posts were not the end of my relationship with this topic, and I began a more in-depth study.

I set out to write a study named something along the lines of *Recognizing and Overcoming Enemy Tactics*. As I studied, I could see enemy tactics wrapping up with the completion of Nehemiah's wall. I chose to let this be the boundary for this study, and I found much more than enemy tactics when I took a closer look. As I dove into Nehemiah's story, I was blown away by the first six chapters.

I'll be honest—I was also a bit challenged, especially by chapter three. Chapter three discusses the rebuilding of the wall around Jerusalem. This chapter reports who built and where on the wall they worked. I was initially stumped about how to proceed. I considered glossing over it, but then I decided to look up all the names and places, and what I found still amazes me. I am confident it will amaze and inspire you, too. Only God can place a story like this in a seemingly mundane section of Scripture.

The book of Nehemiah is located between Ezra and Esther in the Bible. However, this is not the chronological sequence of events. The historical order of the books is Ezra, Esther, and Nehemiah. Knowing this progression gives us insight into Nehemiah as he sets out on his God adventure. He would have carried with him an understanding of God's faithfulness to Ezra and Esther. All three lived during the Persian Empire. Nehemiah's king succeeded Esther's husband, Xerxes or Ahasuerus.

This eight-week study begins in Persia, where Nehemiah was concerned for his homeland. As he prayed, a dream developed in his heart—a dream only God could accomplish. He continued praying until a door of opportunity opened to him. As with Esther, his request put his life at risk. But instead of dying, he found himself on a journey, as he walked out God's master plan for his life. His passion for God's kingdom drew him out of the life he knew and sent him on what I have come to call a God-adventure. He shifts from king's servant to regional governor and foreman of the wall reconstruction in Jerusalem. Nehemiah's surrender to God's will for his life transitioned him to a position where he could restore both a wall and the hope of a nation.

As you travel with Nehemiah from Susa to Jerusalem and around Jerusalem's wall, you will be inspired to find your passion and to dream big dreams with God. Nehemiah will teach you to recognize enemy tactics and respond appropriately. You will see a beautiful redemption story in Nehemiah's survey of the wall and rejoice in a transformation story as you travel with him during the work. Nehemiah will seek to restore you and connect you to your kingdom passion, with tools to bring your walk to fulfillment, just as God fulfilled Nehemiah's fervor for his people and the restoration of the wall of Jerusalem.

Nehemiah's Passion

DAY ONE

Nehemiah 1–6

To begin our study of Nehemiah, we will read chapters one through six to gain an overview of this study. Do not be overwhelmed, and do not dig in too deep yet. These are relatively short chapters, and we will begin the excavation tomorrow. Write below or on a separate sheet of paper any thoughts or questions you have as you read through these chapters. If this seems too much for your schedule today, read and record what you can.

If you have time, you can choose from a variety of approaches to challenge yourself further. A good tool for Bible study is often to record five observations: sins to avoid, promises to keep/claim, examples to follow, commands to obey, and knowledge about God (S.P.E.C.K.). Another method is to note the who, what, when, where, and why. As mentioned before, another possibility is to write down questions you come up with during your read-through. We will see if those questions get answered as we traverse these chapters together over the next few weeks.

DAY TWO

The first chapter of Nehemiah gives us insight into the character of a man who did great work for the kingdom of God. The story unfolds in Shushan, or Susa, the capital of the Persian Empire, where Nehemiah lived and worked. The text reveals it was the month of Chislev, which ran from mid-November to mid-December. At Nehemiah's request, men from Jerusalem reported on the welfare of those who resided in Jerusalem and the condition of the city.

Years before, Ezra had returned to Jerusalem with other captives and restored the temple. He made a sincere attempt to restore worship in the heart of Israel. Nehemiah was deeply concerned about Ezra's work and how religious life had been progressing. When the men came from Jerusalem, he could not wait to discover the state of his beloved city and its inhabitants who had returned from captivity.

The men were unable to offer a good report. Nehemiah must have longed to hear how Jerusalem was alive with restored worship and reverence for God. Unfortunately, their report was of "great distress and reproach" in the province (Nehemiah 1:3). They also noted the sad state of Jerusalem's wall, which was broken down, its gates burned.

The Hebrew word for *distress* translates as "great evil."[i] *Distress* or *affliction* can mean "moral deficiencies" or "below par."[ii] *Reproach* means "injuries from enemies."[iii]

Fast-forward to today's culture and see beautiful, ornate church buildings doing the business of church, surrounded by worldly companies and compromising Christians. It just became relevant, didn't it? We live in a similar culture. Yes, churches do exist where the Spirit of God is alive and active, but the Church has been in great peril. The Church has been complacent with compromise, and the world has a more substantial influence than the body of Christ in our culture. Christians are easily mocked on television, whether in the media or on a sitcom. Today, the Church is in great distress and reproach. If you do not agree with this statement, maybe you will at least agree it is not far from true. I also believe we are on the verge of a turnaround, just as Jerusalem would be, with Nehemiah's help.

The temple represents our hearts before the Lord, our worship centers. We ask Jesus to come into our hearts, and this is where He resides upon the throne of our lives if we allow Him access. The walls of Jerusalem are the boundaries we set to guard our temples—our hearts. We ensure we are not compromised in our faith walk with Jesus. We must be diligent in keeping our walls and gates secure.

How do you see today's culture in comparison to Nehemiah's day?

How are you diligent in keeping the walls and gates to your worship center (your heart for Jesus) secure?

The moment Nehemiah heard of the distress and reproach of the people of God, he sat down, wept, prayed, and fasted—for many days. Verses 4 through 11 record Nehemiah's prayer before the Lord, which he prayed night and day for many days. He prayed unceasingly. *Unceasingly* does not mean it was one long prayer-and-fasting marathon. It means he continued his daily chores in a reverent state before the Lord, praying in his inner man when appropriate and using words when it was safe.

What drives you to weep, fast, and pray for the world around you?

How has your compassion for the world around you moved you to action?

Who or what group or circumstance are you moved to tears for?

For whom are you willing to pray and fast for many days? What moves your heart with compassion?

Your passion will reveal your ministry calling. Give yourself to prayer and fasting and see what the Lord will do. Pray until He opens a door, then boldly walk through it. Prayerfully ponder this today and write below what you feel the Holy Spirit is highlighting for you. Tomorrow we will take a closer look at Nehemiah's prayer.

Days Three and Four

Nehemiah 1:4–11

Look at Nehemiah's prayer and outline his steps in praying to God.

Nehemiah prayed to the God of Heaven, which is the God of Hosts or God of Armies. He called Him great and awesome, "able to do mighty acts; terrible, able to inflict the heaviest judgments."[iv] The Covenant Keeper to those who love and obey Him, He is merciful, the God who forgives. To experience His promises and covenant-keeping ways, you must love and follow Him.

Write John 14:15.

How do you react to this scripture? Does it feel like an ominous command from a distant God or an invitation to intimacy by a loving Savior?

Nehemiah began to confess sin only after he praised God (by ascribing attributes and humbling himself). Interestingly, he did not confess only his own sins but also the sins of his fathers and all Israel. Confessing others' sins might seem strange, but Isaiah, Jeremiah, Daniel, and others did the same (Isaiah 64:6–7; Jeremiah 3:24–25; Daniel 9:20). Recognizing Israel as a theocracy—a government whose head is God—allows us to see this as praying and confessing the sins of the Church as well as those of the nation. A biblical precedent exists for both.

When Nehemiah reminded God of His promises, he confirmed and bolstered his own faith in those promises. He recounted God's promise to scatter Israel, the situation they were in then, and reminded Him of His promise to gather them again. I do not think God needed reminding. He is not forgetful. However, Nehemiah's faith and request for God to fulfill the promise is an example worth noting. We pray the promises of God, not because they remind Him but because they remind us and bolster our faith and hope.

In verse 10, Nehemiah reminds God of His covenant relationship with Israel and His ability to save. He prays God's favor for the remnant who desire to follow Him—the repentant.

What inspires or challenges you about Nehemiah's prayer? How might it affect your prayer life going forward?

NEHEMIAH 1:4–11

Describe Nehemiah's relationship with the king. How does this compare/contrast to our relationship with King Jesus?

Nehemiah was the king's cupbearer; however, he was more than a simple wine taster. Nehemiah's job was akin to a butler, but a butler with extras. He would undoubtedly have been the keeper of the wine, but he would also have had dealings with the king's finances. He would have been a friend and confidant of the king, albeit a servant-confidant. He could lose his position and even his life, if he were to displease his king. It was not a friendship as we know it by any means.[v]

Nehemiah prayed for three months, and then, one day, the king asked him what troubled him – the door opened. Nehemiah was able to state his case to the king, and the king granted his entire request for traveling mercies, supplies, and letters of support to rebuild the wall of Jerusalem. Because Nehemiah prayed and waited, he could say he knew the hand of his God was on the open door. Knowing God's hand is on your ministry is enough to keep you going when it becomes challenging. When others begin to speak against you or do not support what you are doing, you can fall back on the knowledge of God's favor on your work. At times, it is all you need; at other times, it is all you have. We will look at this over the next few days.

I hope the example of Nehemiah's passion, prayer, and providence inspires you to go with God's purpose in your heart. If you have not found your passion yet or are unsure, begin to notice what moves you. Whether you see it on the news or on the street, pray into it. Find out what Scripture says or the promises attached to it, then pray, pray, pray, and wait for God to open the door. This does not mean to sit on the couch and wait for someone to knock on your door to invite you. I suppose that could happen, but it is not likely. Be willing to step out, but only in God's timing. It also does not mean you cannot serve other ministries until you find your place of calling. You might find it as you step out to support others. I pray you will find what makes you passionate for the kingdom and the avenue God has ordained for you to fulfill it.

How do you know when God's hand is in or on your circumstances?

Why is it important to know God's hand is on you for a specific purpose?

What passion has God placed in your heart? What are you doing to partner with it? In what ways have you struggled with this purpose/passion?

DAY FIVE

NEHEMIAH 2:1–2

Three months separate chapters one and two of Nehemiah. According to the Hebrew calendar, Chislev is the ninth month, and Nisan is the first. While it looks pretty fluid as we read through chapters one and two, it is imperative to note the length of time between these two chapters. When we do this, we understand Nehemiah did not receive an instant answer to his prayer. Instead, Nehemiah had been praying for his beloved Jerusalem for months as we transition from chapter one to chapter two.

Why is it important to note the time between chapters 1 and 2?

We see the result of Nehemiah's heartfelt prayers as he stood before the king and queen with a sorrowful countenance (Nehemiah 2:1). Nehemiah placed himself in genuine danger when he allowed himself to have a sorrowful countenance in the presence of his king. Ancient depictions of court servants in the Persian kingdom often show them covering their mouths with their hands, as if to erase or hide any expression. On the other hand, they may have been required to have joyful expressions amid their royals to suggest joy in serving them.[vi] If this was the case, we must understand Nehemiah's courage in allowing his countenance to reveal his heart in the king's sight.

Why might Nehemiah have feared sharing his heart with his king-friend?

Do you ever have trouble sharing your heart with your King-Friend? Why or why not?

As stated, Nehemiah's relationship with the king, as his wine taster, involved much more than checking his wine for poison. Nehemiah would also have managed the king's finances and been his companion—a subjugated companion, rather than a friend at ease. Nehemiah's position was one of access to the king but not one of privilege.[vii] Therefore he prayed and waited for God to reveal His timing.

We see how well the king knew Nehemiah when the king discerned Nehemiah's condition as sorrow of the heart rather than illness.[viii] Scripture does not tell us whether Nehemiah meant for the king to see his emotion or if it just welled up at this inopportune time. However, Nehemiah's "becoming dreadfully afraid" (2:2) gives us a clue about his motives. His fear suggests he knew advocating for Jerusalem to the king could endanger his life, due to Jerusalem's reputation as a rebellious city. Either way, the king noticed and asked Nehemiah to explain his sorrow.

Nehemiah stood before his questioning king, knowing the previous king's acts. Artaxerxes I (or Ahasuerus) had halted the building in Jerusalem in Ezra's time due to reports of rebellion (Ezra 4).[ix] Therefore, Nehemiah was careful not to mention the place of which he spoke until he could no longer avoid it.

Read Esther 2:1-10; 4:14-5:7; and 7:1-6. How is this Artaxerxes I (Ahasuerus) related to Esther, and how does Nehemiah's circumstance relate to Esther's story?

How might Esther's testimony have helped Nehemiah? How do their stories help you?

Esther's story began with Mordecai's advising her to conceal her ancestry as the Persians sought her for the king's harem (Esther 2:10). She obeyed her uncle. Then she found herself in a position to save all of Israel. Esther risked her life when she entered her husband's throne room without being summoned. Next Esther found herself sitting with her king at a banquet she served (Esther 5:4–7; 7:2). She is credited for being the first Jew to complete a courageous act in the presence of a Persian king. She entered the throne room without invitation (Esther 5:1, 2). One has to wonder if Nehemiah's knowledge of her courage bolstered him on this day.

Nehemiah's Passion Turns to Action

WEEK TWO / DAY ONE

Nehemiah 2:3–20

NEHEMIAH 2:3–8

Nehemiah recognized the open door. But rather than barreling headlong through it with his heart laid bare, he took a careful approach. He began by giving the king respect: "May the king live forever!" (Nehemiah 2:3). Then, directly and honestly, he invited the king to understand and experience his emotion. Nehemiah showed the qualities of a good leader by not laying out the big vision all at once. Instead, he gave it in bite-size pieces, probably for two reasons. First, to see if the king would be interested in knowing more, and second, to see if it displeased the king. For one, he could provide more; for the other, he could adjust his direction. He would not want to overwhelm the king with information, and he left room for escape if the king was not receptive. His wise decision bore fruit when the king showed interest and asked for more.

In response to Nehemiah's emotional expression of concern for his ancestral graves and homeland, the king immediately sought to know Nehemiah's desire: "What do you request?" (Nehemiah 2:4). The king's invitation for his wine-tasting companion to make a request is surprising. Nehemiah had been praying for months. He had been wrestling with God over His call—the impossible task—and the absurdity of a wine-taster's turning builder. Nevertheless, here he was, in the moment, door open wide before him.

How did Nehemiah display the qualities of a good leader? What can you take from this to apply to your own life?

Have you been there? Have you been praying for what is on your heart or feeling drawn to an activity over your head, a too-big-for-you calling, and suddenly found yourself at a door of opportunity? What did you do? What would you do?

Here is what Nehemiah did: Nehemiah shot an arrow prayer right into the heart of God. He cried out quickly and quietly to His God for help, knowing he was standing in a divinely appointed moment. Psalm 37:4 tells us that God gives us the desires of our hearts when we delight in Him. This does not mean He grants us every wish we have. Instead, it reveals that when we lift Him up, He places desires in our hearts beyond what we would ever dream for ourselves. Then, just as with Nehemiah, He sets a plan in motion to fulfill those desires with better dreams than we could come to on our own (Ephesians 3:20). One truth we can take away from this moment in Nehemiah's story is that God will answer the arrow prayer lifted from a sincere and submitted heart.

In this moment, does Nehemiah come to the end of his wrestling, or has he been on board the whole time? How often has God called you to serve in ways you could not do alone? Nehemiah was a money guy, a wine guy, and a sequestered friend. He was not a city governor, nor was he a builder. Nevertheless, Nehemiah did not let what he was not keep him from becoming what he could be with a little—okay, a lot—of divine assistance. Nehemiah expressed this in his prayer: If You get me there, I will build it. Then he gave the king the goal of rebuilding the city wall of his homeland.

What does "God gives us the desires of our hearts" mean? Was this definition a new thought for you? How will you respond to the desires of your heart from now on?

What would you do for God's kingdom if money and qualifications were not an issue?

To what is God calling you? Do you see how Nehemiah spent months in prayer over it? Are you praying into the vision God has given you? Do you believe He will equip you to do whatever He calls you to (Hebrews 13:20–21; 1 Peter 5:10)? If not, why not? Will you courageously pray, "Yes, Lord; send me, and I will go?" The greatest adventure on earth comes when we say yes to the King of kings and Lord of lords.

Finding himself in the king's favor, Nehemiah stepped through the open door and laid out his request—in detail. He seemed to garner courage as he laid it out to the king. He sensed the Lord's hand upon him and asked the king for the moon—and the king gave it to him.

Through his discourse with the king, Nehemiah teaches us how to relate with our King. First, Nehemiah approached his king with reverence. He had a healthy fear of his king and gave him the honor due his name. We, too, must approach our King with reverence and worship. He deserves all glory, honor, and praise, so do not hold it back. Beginning a discourse with God is best when soaked in praise and worship. It helps us align ourselves, with Him on the throne and our hearts humbled before Him.

Nehemiah said, "If it pleases the king" (Nehemiah 2:7). Our prayers ought always to be seasoned with the desire for our requests to be pleasing to God. The posture of surrender is how we know our hearts are right before Him when we come to Him with our requests—when we can say, "If it pleases You, Lord, then hear my prayer." However, if our hearts are not right in our requests, if we are coming for selfish gain, we will know it, for we will have more difficulty saying, "Your will not mine."

Once Nehemiah knew he stood in the king's favor, he did not leave out a single detail. He released the entire too-big-for-me dream. Nehemiah experienced hope when he knew he had the king's favor. It is the same for us because we know our God is for us and not against us (Romans 8:31). He *does* want to give us the desires of our hearts when we are in line with His will/pleasure. Nehemiah opened up to his king with boldness and authenticity. God wants the same from us. He invites us, in His word, to come boldly to

His throne of grace (Hebrews 4:6). We have an invitation. Do not leave out a single detail. God wants you to ask in detail. He wants you to come as you are and make your requests known to Him through your genuine and authentic self (Philippians 4:6). What could please our Father more than to have us come to Him with our whole, honest self? It is within this space where He can divinely and supernaturally interact with us.

I remember when God told me who my husband would be years before my husband knew. I had some heart-rending times as I traversed the promise in real time. Nevertheless, I trusted God, and for the most part, I did very well in the waiting. The most challenging part of the waiting was God's asking me to confess to Him my heart's desire to marry this man.

The lesson I learned in my obedience is this: There are times when we are to accept God's will passively, and other times we must agree with God's will through our confession. It was far riskier to say out loud, "God, I want to marry this man," than it was to say, "Yes, Lord, if this is the man you have for me, I accept him." Do you see the difference? Once I confessed my heart's desire, I owned it, and losing it would be much more devastating. I married him in 1997 after three years of waiting.

Another example of being a detailed pray-er is when I needed a new car, while I was single and money was tight. I asked the Lord which of the men from my singles' group I should take to the auto dealership. I heard Him say in my heart, "If you take someone with you, I will not get the glory."

It made sense, so I prayed for the car I wanted. I asked for four cylinders and four doors, to save money on fuel and insurance. I said I did not need bells and whistles; I could still roll my own windows up, and so on. It was vital for the dealer to give me a certain amount of money back to pay off a bill so I could afford a car payment even though I was looking for used car. I needed them to provide me with an exact amount of money for my trade-in car. I had done my research. I finished the list of items I needed. I added, "Oh, and if you could make it blue, it would be great." Immediately feeling selfish, I apologized.

I went shopping for a new car the day after a devastating flood had saturated the Pacific Northwest. I was the only customer on the lot for about five hours, lunch break included. I met a salesman, and we looked at cars. I told him I needed four cylinders and doors. He took me to the area with the Pontiac Grand Ams. My heart sank a little. I was bringing in a Toyota Tercel—quite a bit of a price difference. I was sure I could not afford a Grand Am, but I went along with him, feeling a divine peace. He would eventually get me to a car I could afford; if not, I could always walk away. We test-drove a green Grand Am with no bells and whistles that met my other criteria.

I took a lunch break and called my bank, and they assured me the price was fair. I went back and began negotiations. It was a used car. My car needed repair. I told them what I needed to get for my car and that I needed cash back and that the car I was buying needed to be no more than so many dollars. I was a fresh-faced twenty-something. They looked dumbfounded by my request, but I was sitting with my God, and I knew I had His favor. I also knew I could walk away from the table at any time.

The first man excused himself and came back with a second man. I reiterated my needs not my requests. They left and came back with more men. I was sitting in a chair in a sterile office with five men, four salesmen and the manager, all standing and bearing down on me. They agreed to give me every bit of what I asked. I knew my God was with me. However, in my heart, I said, "But, Lord, it isn't blue." A pang of guilt washed through me, and I apologized—again.

Soon a man returned to the room and said, "I am very sorry, but there seems to be an issue with the car. Come take a look." I was amazed to see dents all over the top of the car and the trunk. It looked like someone had taken a baseball bat to it. I assure you I had looked the car over carefully before I test drove it, and there was not a scratch on it. I knew God was in it.

The man apologized and said, "We have another Grand Am comparable to this one. It is newer and has fewer miles. The only problem is, it is blue. Is that okay?" I shared an internal smile with the Lord as praise lifted from my heart to my good God. I accepted their offer and went to look at it. It was a pale baby blue, and my heart sank, as I said to the Lord, "It's not the right shade of blue." Again with the guilt and the repentance. I was starting to become quite disappointed with myself and my ungrateful attitude. I went back to wait some more and tried to convince the Lord (and myself) that I was grateful.

The man returned and told me there was also an issue with the second car. The window seals had failed, and the torrential rains had filled it up to the seats with rainwater. He said not to worry, "We have one more Grand Am. It is a fleet car with six thousand fewer miles, is a few years newer, and has power locks, windows, and more." It had all the bells and whistles, and it was royal blue—the right blue.

My sales guy was so happy for me. He took me to the car and practically gushed as he showed me all the little blessings the Lord had just bestowed upon me. My great God's kindness toward me and His attention to detail amazed me. I realized then how important it is to pray specifically, even if merely to watch the miraculous hand of my God move on my behalf. By the way, my scripture verse for the day was, "Now to Him who is able to do exceedingly abundantly above all that we ask or think, according to the power that works in us" (Ephesians 3:20). The verse following is appropriate, too: "To Him be glory in the church by Christ Jesus to all generations, forever and ever. Amen" (Ephesians 3:21).

Nehemiah brought his requests boldly to this earthly king's throne, knowing his heavenly King's hand was upon him. He asked to be released from his duties to rebuild his ancestral home. He asked for letters for safe passage and needed supplies for the building project. Nehemiah also received protection and honor in the form of a military escort and the title of governor. He was honest and bold and received all he asked for and more.

What have you been afraid to ask of the Lord? What part have you been hiding from Him—as if He does not already know it is there? He is able to meet you where your authentic self is willing to come to Him. Will you come to Him and lay your requests out before Him, knowing you are in His favor, knowing He will meet you at your authentic self, and knowing He will only give you His best?

I hope you can see how Nehemiah's benefits with the Persian king mirror our own with our Lord and King. Nehemiah had the king's favor. If you have received Jesus as your Lord and Savior, you stand in favor before your eternal King. Nehemiah changed his station from cup-bearer to governor. We trade our slave clothes for the garments of kings and priests (1 Peter 2:9). He left his mundane life to build the wall of Jerusalem, an Old Testament kingdom work. We trade our aimless life for a life of purpose, building the kingdom of God. Nehemiah lived in one kingdom but worked for another. We live on earth in the secular world, but we are not of this world; we live for and work for a higher kingdom and purpose (John 18:36).

Nehemiah went with letters bearing the king's seal guaranteeing safe passage and supplies. God promises to guide and protect us as well as meet our needs. Finally, Nehemiah received a detachment of military personnel to accompany him and provide Him with further protection beyond what the letters commanded. We are given divine protection we cannot see in the heavenly realm. We live in a spiritual world where the unseen battle rages around us and on our behalf. We must trust in His divine protection and supply when we walk in faith and obey our calling.

What is the greatest adventure on earth? Will you say yes today? How?

What spoke to you in the testimonies? Why?

For what do we trade our aimless lives? What does that look like for you?

Will Nehemiah's example change the way you approach your King? Why or why not?

DAY TWO

How did Nehemiah enter Jerusalem? How might this be a foreshadowing of Christ?

Nehemiah had his plan. He gave his letter to Asaph, the keeper of the king's forest, to begin preparing his supplies. He had also given his letters to the governors of the land. Nehemiah did all of this before he ever entered Jerusalem. A dispatch of captains and horsemen of the Persian army having been sent with him, we can expect them to have remained in Jerusalem to protect Nehemiah.

Nehemiah was sent to Jerusalem as governor with a Persian guard. He could have arrived commanding his will, with the king's full authority behind him. He could have carried out the Lord's work with his own power. Instead Nehemiah came humbly into Jerusalem, but he stood with authority against Jerusalem's enemies. He made room for partnership with Israel rather than subjecting its enemies to servitude—humility in leadership.

Three is a powerful number. Three months of prayer preceded the moment with the king that had brought Nehemiah to Jerusalem. When he arrived, he rested and waited three days for His God—a mark of a mature saint who knows who truly is in charge (Zechariah 4:6). He could have rushed in, puffed up with his agenda. Instead he chose the quiet approach.

One might think Nehemiah would go immediately to the elders/leaders of Jerusalem with his good news of the king's favor to rebuild. He might come in his excitement at what the Lord had done, was doing, and was about to do and want to offer immediate relief to those they were called and sent to help. However, Nehemiah showed us a better way. Nehemiah rested for three days upon his arrival, telling no one of his plans. The number three is not a coincidence or a mistake in Scripture. Yes, Nehemiah had just finished a long journey from his Persian king to Jerusalem and probably needed a bath and a rest. However, I do not think this is all there was to it. If we look at the threes in Scripture, we often see three as a number preceding the mighty acts of God.

What better way did Nehemiah show us? Why is this a better way?

Look up the following scriptures and note what you learn about the number three: Joshua 1:11; 3:2–17

Jonah 1:17; 3:3–10

Matthew 12:40; Luke 24:45-48

The number three represents the smallest complete cycle. Three is the first plural number because two is considered a dual.[i] Through Jesus's death and resurrection, we see the number three as a complete cycle. R. L. Harris says of the power of the number three, "Man's sin was fully judged, yet grace triumphed."[ii] While we could go on to many more examples in Scripture of the number three preceding mighty acts of God, these examples are enough to accept the validity of this claim.

Whether Nehemiah planned it this way or not, we cannot believe it to be a coincidence. We must trust God in the waiting. I love Graham Cooke's statement, "Rest is a weapon."[iii] Nehemiah was about to embark on a mission for the Lord that would garner opposition. He needed to begin with rest—not merely a physical rest, but the rest of the Lord—and faith for the mission. He needed to know who he was in the Lord's plan and to know the able power of God to carry him through.

What did Nehemiah's waiting for three days say about his faith in God?

What enables those in power or leadership to walk humbly in their calling?

Why was rest a vital component of Nehemiah's calling? Describe *rest* in this context.

Where is the Lord telling you to find rest in this season?

What is possible to the one who walks in the confidence and humility of Nehemiah?

What is God calling you to in this season of your life-walk with Him? Are you a frustrated saint who does not understand why you are at a standstill? Have you moved forward ahead of the Lord? Are you moving in rest, or are you conquering your call in your strength?

God says, "Not by might nor by power, but by My Spirit" (Zechariah 4:6). Hear the call of God on your life, but start with prayer and humility. Know you cannot fulfill any work without His hand upon you. Yes, we can accomplish projects and purposes in our power. But they will not last, nor will they have the profound impact they could have if we had waited upon the Lord, knowing He alone brings the victory and to Him alone belongs all the glory, honor, and praise. When we can walk in the confidence and humility of Nehemiah, we will be a people who can build the kingdom without fear of enemy tactics.

I am coming off a long season of rest. I do not think I have done it fully well, but I have learned much. I have learned I will not lose my place in the line of calling or purpose for the Lord. I have learned how rest is a weapon. I have learned to carry rest with me into the work. I have known sober judgment regarding how much is mine to do and how God truly does carry all of the weight. He is the One who draws and changes hearts. He is the One who shows up in a moment and gives me the words someone else needs to hear. Holy Spirit faithfully brings scriptures to mind when someone else needs to hear them. I have learned not to stress over whether or not He will show up. It is for me to be faithful to come to peace with whether He shows up or not because it is truly all about Him and all up to Him. Rest—it is a weapon. Wield it.

DAY THREE

NEHEMIAH 2:12–16

The following curious thing we see Nehemiah do is go out by night to assess the damage to the wall. It seems so strange unless we consider his situation. He was coming in with letters from a Persian king. A guard of Persian soldiers accompanied him. He was coming to a place he loved but to a people who did not know him or his heart for God, them, or their city. He went with a mind to restore the seat of Israel, the place of their God and kings, the location from which they had ruled their part of the world. Jerusalem had always had enemies, and Nehemiah was no fool. He did not assume the hand of his God upon him negated his responsibility to do his part. As a good leader, he needed to understand the why, what, and how before he could inspire others to follow his vision.

Nehemiah set out to survey the job ahead. One's vision for the call can often be vastly different from the activity of the call—setting hands and feet to work. Nehemiah was at the cusp of his vision's becoming a reality. He was about to see what he had been praying for come to fruition.

I have experienced this. Have you? Every time I am inspired to do a work for the Lord—even write this study—it always turns out to be more work and labor than I thought it would be in the inception. We tend to romanticize ideals. Counting the cost before we set out is vital to ensure we finish well (Luke 14:27–32). Scholar A. J. Wenham says of Nehemiah, "In an unsecure environment he needed to find the solid ground of truth as soon as possible. Only then could he disclose what he believed to be the God-given task of rebuilding the wall."[iv]

What challenges did Nehemiah face? Why would this be of concern? How can you apply this to your own life and walk with Christ?

Why is it important to count the cost before embarking on the journey?

Nehemiah recorded the names of the gates and areas he passed in his nighttime journey. According to the New King James Version, Nehemiah's journey touched the Valley Gate, the Serpent Well, the Refuse (or Dung) Gate, the Fountain Gate, and the King's Pool. When he could go no further, he turned and went back through the Valley Gate (Nehemiah 2:13, 14).

Many historians say the Valley Gate connects to the Valley of Hinnom. The Valley of Hinnom and the Valley of Kidron meet in the south. Nehemiah's travels connected him to both valleys. He began at Kidron, where Molech worship took place. The Valley of Hinnom was also where garbage and dead animals were brought and burned.[v] According to the New Illustrated Bible Dictionary (NIBD), "Hinnom . . . became a graphic symbol of woe and judgment and the place of eternal punishment called Hell." The Greek translation is Gehenna.[vi] This was the beginning position of Nehemiah's journey around the wall of Jerusalem. This site would remind him of the judgment of God, which had landed Judah in exile.

The next place mentioned is the Serpent Well. The word for "serpent" also translates from Hebrew as "dragon or jackal, sea monster, serpent, or whale."[vii] *Well*, here, "designates a flow of water from an opening in a hillside or valley."[viii] It may also mean "source."[ix] Lying as it does between the Valley Gate associated with the Valley of Hinnom and the Refuse or Dung Gate, I am not sure this is the well from which I want to drink or find refreshment.

As you may have guessed, the Refuse Gate descends into the Valley of Hinnom discussed above.[x] The name translates as "ash heap" or "refuse," and the reasons why are apparent.[xi] Nehemiah's survey revealed both gates burned, like the refuse in the Valley of Hinnom, along with heaps of ash (Nehemiah 2:13).

Continuing beyond the Refuse Gate, Nehemiah arrived at the Fountain Gate on the eastern side of Jerusalem. The original word for *fountain* translates as "eye." What is interesting is the context for how this word translates. This water source is understood to be the mouth of the Fountain of Siloah, which feeds the King's Pool.[xii] Let us take it further and realize that *mouth* here refers to another "source" of water. (We will come back to this in tomorrow's notes.) The Hebrew word for *fountain* or *eye* also translates as: "growing dim, open after sleep, of new power of vision, given by God, giving sight to the blind, opening his eyes, reviving, and apple of the eye, to name a few."[xiii] If you are a bit of a Bible scholar, I think you might see where we are going with this.

The King's Pool was the farthest point of Nehemiah's venture around the wall. It is appropriate for what we see in this context of the places he has traveled. The King's Pool, also known as the Virgin's Well, is where Hezekiah cut the conduit to take water from the spring to the Pool of Siloam.[xiv] This pool, literally translates as "a bursting forth,"[xv] the verb closely related is "break forth, of light, etc."[xvi] This pool is where the Light of the World, Jesus, sent a man to wash his eyes and receive his healing (John 9:7,11). The Greek translation is "sent."

What is symbolized at the Valley Gate?

How does this relate to Nehemiah's journey? How does this relate to your journey?

Between what two sites does the Serpent's Well reside?

Would this be a well of refreshing? Why or why not?

How might you apply this to your life and where your source resides?

What does Refuse/Dung Gate translate as, and how does this compare to the wall of Jerusalem?

How would one who lingers in this area begin to feel and act? How does this apply to your life?

What foreshadowing(s) of Christ do you see in this Fountain Gate? For which are you most grateful? How does this speak to you so far?

What is special about this being the farthest point of Nehemiah's nighttime journey?

What is historically significant about this location?

How might this relate to a salvation story? Ponder this, and we will discuss it more tomorrow.

DAY FOUR

NEHEMIAH 2:12–16

Today we will look at Nehemiah's wall walk in terms of spiritual application. Nehemiah's walk was one of a man returning from captivity, a captivity brought on by God's judgment of Judah's sin. Consider what we learned about the places Nehemiah walked past yesterday. Today I will lead with the questions so you can ponder and listen to Holy Spirit. I wish I could be there to hear you share your revelations. Please personalize your answers to the following questions as much as possible.

To what can we relate Nehemiah's starting place?

How does Satan come at us today? Of what does he want to convince us?

What is one sign that tells us we are seeking satisfaction in the wrong places?

Where does the Dung/Refuse Gate lead?

What is the choice each person has at the Dung Gate?

What does the Fountain Gate represent spiritually?

Where does it come from, and how can we spiritually apply this?

How do we come to this place of refreshing?

What comes after the Fountain Gate? Apply this.

What is significant about Nehemiah's having to dismount?

Nehemiah's walk around Jerusalem began in the west at the place related to hell and the eternal burning of garbage and flesh. It relates scripturally to the final judgment.

Nehemiah moved from the place of hell and judgment toward the Serpent's Well, a source of water coming from the hillside or valley, which is associated with eternal fire. Satan is the serpent of Genesis who deceived the woman and man, bringing us all to live in a condition of sin (Genesis 3:1–19). We each need to deal with sin to avoid eternal fire. Satan is a source of lies and temptation. Although this source of water seems to be a place to satisfy thirst, its source is the very pit of hell. Satan comes to us, just as he did to Adam and Eve, and attempts to convince us he is a source of satisfaction. But he only gives a counterfeit satisfaction, lasting but a moment and passing into the wretchedness of life. Nehemiah passed by this counterfeit source toward the Dung Gate.

The Dung Gate is the doorway to the source of all lies and the eternal flames of hell—the crossroad. One can go through this gate, meet the source of lies, and spend eternity in flame or turn and go in the other direction—the direction Nehemiah traveled. We are either traveling toward hell or toward heaven. No other path will be found, and we do not stand still. Let's keep going!

Nehemiah passed through the Dung Gate and arrived at the Fountain Gate—from filth into a place of cleansing and refreshing. The Fountain Gate sources the King's Pool; it comes from another place to source this place. Jesus, our Source of Life, comes from another place, but He is our True Source. He cleanses us from all unrighteousness; we have only to go to Him.

Look up the following verses and record how they apply in the context of Nehemiah's walk.

1 John 1:9

John 14:6

What did Peter say of Jesus in Acts 4:12?

This source feeds the King's Pool, the place of healing. He is the way to the Father—which brings us to the King's Pool. The King's Pool is where the road narrowed, forcing Nehemiah to dismount and go on foot.

Write Jesus's words from Matthew 7:13–14:

Just as the Fountain Gate leads to the King's Pool, Jesus is the gate leading to the Father. The Pool of Siloam in the New Testament is akin to the King's Pool of Nehemiah's experience. It is a place where one goes to find healing. To find salvation in Jesus is to be redeemed, delivered, and protected. Jesus truly is the Way, the Truth, and the Life. Here we have two gates: one to hell and one to salvation.

Where are you on this journey Nehemiah prophetically walked for you? To which gate are you standing closer? In which direction are you traveling?

The good news is Jesus will help us get through the narrow gate and into the pool of healing: (salvation, deliverance, and protection) if we cry out to Him. He went to the cross to make this possible for all who would call on Him (John 3:16). If you have cried out to Him, you can count on Him to come through for you.

Look up Hebrews 12:2 and state why this truth is sure for us.

Nehemiah prophetically walked out the salvation story. He also prophetically walked out the restoration of Jerusalem, from captivity to physical return to Jerusalem and Israel. He, along with Esther and Ezra, was used by God to open a way for His wayward ones to come home, just as He promised. Nehemiah's prophetic walk holds a message for us today.

We must walk our salvation-walk with Jesus on our own. It is a walk for the individual; it is personal and intimate. Nehemiah gave himself to this journey before inviting anyone else to join him. How about you? Have you taken this journey with Jesus? Whom have you told about it? Will you tell someone this week? Ask God to point out someone with whom you can share your story.

How has Nehemiah's journey around the wall ministered to you? Are there changes you will make based on this?

Do you agree or disagree with the statement about two paths? Why or why not? (Support your position with scripture.)

DAY FIVE

Why was Nehemiah wise to determine the need and the "yes" before he presented his plan? How can you apply this to your life/ministry?

Nehemiah was wise in determining the need and the yes before presenting his proposal. How often have you shared, only to have one or more nay-sayers shut you and your idea down? Without doing research or formulating a plan, you will have no answer for them or yourself against these negative responses. Nehemiah walked all of this out before ever mentioning it to anyone (Nehemiah 2:16). In a sense, he walked the walk before he talked the talk. He counted the cost of what he would ask the people to do. He did not walk in with a romanticized idea of the project; he got eyes on it to prepare his heart and mind before sharing the plan—such wisdom. Wise leaders come equipped to inspire others to see and participate in the vision.

Nehemiah brought his plan to a people who had lived with this broken-down wall and these burned gates for decades. They had become accustomed to living this way.

Ask Jesus to reveal any broken walls or gates you may be living with. We can become accustomed to negative patterns of life God has not ordained for us.

Ask the Lord to point out an area He would like to rebuild in your life. He does not want you living with broken walls or burned gates. Come to Him with the faith and trust of a child and allow Him to heal the broken places. If you trust Him enough to allow Him access, He is gentle and kind and will bring you to completion.

Sometimes we need someone outside our usual circles to point out our blind spots. We can have an unseen burned gate or a broken wall. Nehemiah was this guy for those living in Jerusalem. He came from outside and could see the damage for what it was. He could inspire those living with it to hope for and dream of a better existence (Nehemiah 2:17).

Nehemiah used a word translated as "reproach" in the New King James Version of the Bible. They had been living under scorn for so long it became ordinary to walk in it. Nehemiah came and suggested there was a better way. By building the wall, they could put away the reproach.[xvii] They could once again walk with heads held high, knowing to whom they belonged.

Why can you bring your broken places to God? How does this relate to putting away scorn or reproach in your life?

How did Nehemiah's preparation pay off?

Why is testimony so important?

Write the names of the three enemies we met in these verses and what you learn about them.

How might Nehemiah's story inspire us to overcome every enemy tactic?

What did it mean when Sanballat and Tobiah were "deeply disturbed" (Nehemiah 2:10)?

How does this relate to 2 Corinthians 10:3–6 and Ephesians 6:12?

What progressive tactics did Nehemiah's enemies employ?

Why might accusations of rebellion be a severe threat? (See Ezra 4:21.)

Moses sent men into the Promised Land with instructions to spy it out and bring back some of the fruit of the land. Only two of those men brought back a positive report, excited about the hand of the Lord, which they saw in the fruit of the land (Numbers 13:1-33). Nehemiah came and spied out the wall by night and brought the fruit of his testimony of God's goodness to him thus far. Nehemiah recounted his story, from hearing of Jerusalem's condition to his conversation and provision of the king to his arrival before them. Nehemiah's preparation paid off in his ability to draw others into his vision and purpose to rebuild the wall.

Testimony is essential for this reason. Our reports inspire others to look for and see His goodness in their lives. It will help them look for and expect Him daily. Testifying to God's goodness also allows us to respond with thanksgiving and praise.

What recent example of the Lord's goodness can you share with someone this week?

Nehemiah's story is one of my many favorites in the Bible. Nehemiah's courage and tenacity met opposition all along the way. A beautiful revelation lies within this story. I like to call it "the tactics of the enemy." As we go through this study, you will see Israel's enemies progressively oppose the building of Jerusalem's wall. You will see an unmistakable likeness to our enemy in these pages of Scripture. In chapter two, we meet the three main characters representing a clear and present opposition to kingdom building: Sanballat the Horonite, Tobiah the Ammonite, and Geshem the Arab.

Sanballat's name reflects his area of residence, inside the former territory of Ephraim. He most likely lived in Beth Horon, which was part of Samaria at this time.[xviii]

Evidence discovered in a Jewish settlement in Egypt referred to Sanballat as the governor of Samaria.[xix] His daughter married the son of the high priest.[xx] This marriage was against God's law and may have been arranged by Sanballat as a power play (Deuteronomy 7:3). Nehemiah dealt with this in the latter part of the book (Nehemiah 13:28).

The Ammonite, Tobiah, was an Ammonite official probably equal in stature to Sanballat, the Samarian governor.[xxi] He was most definitely similar to him in his disdain for Israel. His position would have made him an official of the Persian king, making him Nehemiah's equal.[xxii] While Tobiah was an expert on the culture and happenings in and around Judah, Nehemiah was the king's cupbearer. The Persian king knew Nehemiah well and had put his trust in him. Therefore, whatever favor Tobiah may have had with Artaxerxes was trumped by Nehemiah's relationship with the king and, more importantly, by the hand of God.

Geshem the Arab was connected to the king of Persia by an alliance. Not only did he lead a confederation of Arab groups, but he was also a king—the king of Qedar, located on Judah's eastern and southern borders.[xxiii] These three men sought to stop the cupbearer from fulfilling his God-given call. Pay attention to these three as you read through the book of Nehemiah and note the progressive steps they take against him. Then see these tactics of the enemy in your own life if you can. One detail is clear: These opposers of the Lord's plan, conveyed through a story of good versus evil, ought to inspire us to overcome every tactic of the enemy just as Nehemiah did.

We first see Sanballat and Tobiah in verse 10. They caught wind of someone trying to do good for the children of God, and they were "deeply disturbed." The original language for *disturbed* speaks of evil; figuratively, it means "to make or be good for nothing."[xxiv] Their reaction to Nehemiah was emotive, compelling them toward evil action. It was immediately in their hearts to thwart Nehemiah's efforts, and they would progressively attempt to end his dream and call.

Our enemy, the devil, "walks about like a roaring lion, seeking whom he may devour" (1 Peter 5:8). He is disturbed by every movement in the kingdom. He is constantly looking for an opportunity to destroy the work of heaven. The good news is that he is already defeated. We, like Nehemiah, need to learn to walk our walk from victory to victory.

Our subsequent encounter with Sanballat and Tobiah is in verse 19, along with Geshem. They began by being disturbed (motivated) by Nehemiah's actions. We witnessed the first progression as they incited others to join their evil plot. Then they progressed to mocking Nehemiah and those who stood with him. We see this more and more in our culture today as Christians are increasingly mocked on television shows, in the news, and face to face. It is a tactic of the enemy. We must keep these actions separate from the people he uses to fulfill his evil plan against us. Our battle is not against flesh and blood (2 Corinthians 10:3–6; Ephesians 6:12).

Nehemiah's enemies progressed from mockery to posing a severe threat not unlike Ezra's experience with them (Ezra 4:1-24). Finally, they accused Nehemiah of attempting to rebel against the king. A similar accusation had stopped Ezra's building project (Ezra 4:21). It was psychological warfare, the battle waged in the mind—the threats, the what-ifs. However, it was a grave accusation and the last tactic the enemy found effective.

Satan is a created being, not a creative one. He has only so many tricks in his bag, the number one being lies. The temptation of Jesus recorded in Luke's gospel reveals this truth. Satan has only so many schemes available.

What do you learn about this from Luke 4:14? What comfort do you find in this knowledge?

I thoroughly believe this: if Satan discovers a tactic that stops you short of God's plan for you, he will use it repeatedly until it no longer works. Then he will move to the next tactic or go away and wait for another chance. I very much want you to see this. When he had done all he had to do, he left Jesus alone "to wait for an opportune time."

Satan will wait and watch for an opportunity to trip you up. When you are too tired, stressed, busy, or hungry, he will step in with a suggestion. You can either agree with it or see it for what it is and brush him off in Jesus's name. Glory to glory, victory to victory is how we win against an enemy who has only so many tricks at his disposal. At the same time, we serve an infinitely creative God and good Father! We overcome by knowing Scripture and keeping our eyes on Jesus and His plans and purposes.

Satan is a created being, not a _____.

The accusation of rebellion came because it was the last tactic that had worked against the building of Jerusalem, so it was the first tool they used against Nehemiah. However, they found Nehemiah to be confident in his calling, with the hand of his God upon him. How is our enemy seeing you today? Are you walking in the assurance of a good Father who has your back? Or are you fearful He is not genuinely watching over you as He promised?

Nehemiah did not seem to look to his training or his station. He relied on a few tools to resist intimidation by these men of foreign interests. He, first of all, knew his king more intimately than they. He knew he had prayed this through for months and seen the hand of God bring him thus far. He knew God was in it; no scheme could come against His excellent plan for His people. Nehemiah seemed to have understood his calling. Success had little more to do with him than saying "yes" and taking one step after another, watching God fulfill his vision before his eyes. Nehemiah also knew, maybe with a small amount of personal pleasure, how the Persian bodyguard the king had sent with him held back these oppositional forces.[xxv] Perhaps the king knew the officials of the local area better than they thought.

This second chapter of Nehemiah has many applications to our lives. First Nehemiah prayed and prayed and prayed, and then he waited. Sometimes it takes time—most of the time it takes longer than we would like. We must remain faithful to pray and wait upon the Lord's timing. He will open doors no one can shut. We cannot open doors He has closed or not yet opened (Isaiah 22:22). When we see the door open a crack, we ought to enter with our hearts tuned in to the Lord's timing, plan, and execution. We do not have to jump through the door and spill every detail at once. Taking one simple step at a time, trusting Him to open the door further and light the path before us as we take each step, is an excellent plan. We do not want to rush headlong into an opportunity, but we also do not want to be stuck waiting, never taking a step. Praying is the first step. Seeing and stepping into the God opportunity is the next step.

Nehemiah did not spill out his entire plan at once. He took his time, and when the door was wide open, he laid out his plan in surrender to the Lord's timing; then he trusted. Nehemiah received more than he could have expected. He entered a foreign land with a plan, protection, and provision. The Lord will not send us where He will not provide for our needs. He will give us His plan, protect us, and provide. We only need to step into His plan. Even when the enemy came against Nehemiah, God gave him the wisdom he needed at every turn. Nehemiah kept his head straight by focusing on God's will and plan for him. He continued going forward by remembering how he had gotten this far, then this far, then this far.

Where are you on this journey today? Have you been praying for what seems like forever, waiting on the Lord? It is good to ask, is this request self-minded or kingdom-purposed?

What did Nehemiah's enemies learn about him on this first attempt at intimidation? What gave him confidence?

What possible applications for your life do you see in this chapter? Which one(s) do you plan to implement? How will you go about it?

Nehemiah and the North Wall

Week Three / Day One

Nehemiah 3:1–5

As Bible study goes, this is not an easy chapter. At first glance, it is simply a record of places around the wall of Jerusalem and who worked to repair those areas. However, when we slow down and examine the names and places, a feast of revelation appears before our eyes. As we take our time to observe the people and locations, we understand we are on a journey of inspiration as we discover what God has hand-written all along the wall.

Read Mark 10:42–43. What did Jesus tell His disciples about leadership?

Our first noteworthy fact is where on the wall this record begins and who built there. We learn the first person named is Eliashib, the high priest, whose name means "God will restore," along with his relatives, the priests.[i] How appropriate that the first to be mentioned as we begin our rebuilding journey were the priests led by the high priest himself. It is a beautiful picture of the religious institution's hierarchical structure, not lording it over those they serve.

Read Leviticus 16:1–34. What do you learn about the high priest and the sacrifice?

The beautiful story here is that these ministers of the house of God were first on the wall, setting an example of service and being practically useful to those around them.

The next fact to note is where their work began, at the Sheep Gate. It is where the animals were brought in and cleansed for sacrificial use. Priests performed the ceremonies of sacrifice on behalf of Israel.[ii] The rebuilding and restoration of the wall of Jerusalem began at the point of the sacrifice.

The sacrificial animals came through the Sheep Gate with a purpose: to cleanse Israel of sin. The high priest was the only one who could enter into God's presence on the Day of Atonement to cleanse the sins of the entire nation of Israel (Leviticus 16:1–34). The animal to bear their sins would have entered through this gate.

Read Hebrews 9:7–28 and 10:10. What do you learn? How do these verses apply the sacrifice to today? Are these thoughts new to you? How do you respond to these truths today?

God invites us to enter through the narrow gate, which is Jesus. He is the Way, the Truth, and the Life. No one comes to the Father except through Him (Matthew 7:14; John 14:6). He is our sacrificial Lamb who bore our sins (Hebrews 9:12, 10:10). When we receive His cleansing work, we enter through the narrow gate and meet Him, our sacrificial Lamb and High Priest. Then we begin a journey of sanctification or transformation to become like Christ (Hebrews 9:7–28). We will travel around the wall of our hearts and rebuild good boundaries as we learn to heal, build, and grow in Christ.

It is awe-inspiring to see God ordain the rebuilding of the wall and the location from which the writer began. The place mirrors our journey, rebuilding our lives to look the way Christ originally intended. A friend recently said, "Jesus did not die to forgive your sins alone; He died to restore your destiny." Here our restoration begins, with accepting Jesus as our Savior and being washed clean as we accept His sacrifice on our behalf. It is merely for us to enter through the Sheep Gate, rebuilt by a man named God Will Restore.

Nehemiah's recounting of the work on the wall travels counterclockwise, suggesting an undoing of what had been. We pass the Towers of the Hundred and Hananel, rebuilt by God Will Restore (Eliashib) and the priests. Not much information is available on the Tower of the Hundred or the Tower of Hananel except that their locations are side by side on the north rampart of Nehemiah's wall. Hananel translates as "God has favored."[iii] Therefore, God Will Restore (Eliashib) is working to rebuild where God Has Favored (Hananel). It seems like a biblical principle tucked away in an uninteresting and easily overlooked part of the story; but this is who our God is. He wastes nothing and can place a message and a promise anywhere. We only have to slow down long enough to see it.

Note what you find interesting about Eliashib and these locations. What stands out to you and why?

How does this relate to Jesus and His work for and in you?

Jesus did not die to forgive my sins alone; He died to _____.
How does this statement affect you? How will you respond?

51

How does one obtain life and favor from the Lord? How does this apply to the building of Nehemiah's wall?

Write out Proverbs 8:34–35 and your thoughts about the scripture and how it applies to today's study.

Day Two

Diving into the meaning of Jericho, following the name's roots, we come up with the words "fragrant, blow, breathe, and the figurative meaning of anticipate or enjoy."[iv] It was a new season, filled with anticipation of what the Lord was doing and was going to do. It was a time for joy and expectation. To continue our salvation analogy, the old has passed away, and we are made new in Christ (2 Corinthians 5:17).

Imagine the anticipation and joy felt by the ones who had returned from living under foreign rule; then that of those who had been left behind in Jerusalem and were the poorest of the land. Those in exile had not seen the destruction of the temple and wall; they had only heard of it. They had either lived in a state of complacency or returned to see the devastation. Then picture their hope for the restoration of the wall, the kingdom of Israel—God's kingdom—and His favor. This anticipation and joy must have floated into the atmosphere around them like a beautiful spring fragrance—the fragrance of the favor of God.

Read and summarize the following scriptures:
Colossians 3:9–10

2 Corinthians 2:15

How does the name Jericho relate to what the Lord was doing in Nehemiah's day? How does it relate to us today?

Do you have a date marked on your calendar for your salvation experience? What is your salvation story? Write it down, then share it with someone this week.

Are you feeling anticipation for a new season? Will you share what it is?

ZACCUR SON OF IMRI: BETWEEN MEN OF JERICHO AND THE FISH GATE
NEHEMIAH 3:2

Zaccur built between those whose name means Fragrance (Jericho) and the Fish Gate. His name means "mindful, with the root meaning of to mark or to remember."[v] It was a time in the life of Israel to remember—when God began to restore Israel to her homeland and worship and to build the city wall. It marked a restorative moment in the history of Israel. It was a moment to be mindful of, to take note, and to consider what the Lord might be doing and where He might be taking them.

Another lesson from Mindful (Zaccur) is to be attentive to what the Lord might do in and through our circumstances. Mindful (Zaccur) built at a section of wall between two destination points. His building area was solely for keeping the enemy out.

Mindful (Zaccur) descended from Imri (Wordy).[vi] The obvious joke is that maybe he was mindful because his father was too wordy and he was not often allowed to vocalize. Perhaps this is true, or maybe the many words of his father showed him the importance of mindfulness.

Read Ecclesiastes 2:14 and 5:3 and note Solomon's wisdom. What do you learn from these scriptures, and how might you apply them to your life?

We see Mindful (Zaccur) as a wise/mindful man who completed the task before him; he built his portion of the wall. He shows us we can grow into our destinies, regardless of our parentage. We do not have to emulate their behaviors; we can find our qualities and characteristics in Christ. Jesus restores us to our created purpose and destiny. We can fulfill our calling in Christ, no matter the sins of our past or the lineage from which we descend. We are made free to flourish in and through Jesus, who came to give us life abundant (John 10:10).

Are you more Zaccur (Mindful) or more Imri (Wordy)? How does your personality fit your call to serve?

Where are you today? Are you merely surviving, living in the abundance Jesus promised, or somewhere in between? If you feel you are simply surviving, what steps can you take to move toward abundance?

Where do changes need to come from for you to find the fullness of freedom in Christ? Meet with Him daily; slow down, settle your mind and heart, and listen for Him. If you ask with a humble and surrendered heart, He will give you the answers you seek. He may not give you the answers you want, but He will provide you with what will lead you into His abundance. Take a moment now to sit in His presence.

Day Three

Sons of Hassenaah: The Fish Gate
Nehemiah 3:3

Following Mindful (Zaccur) son of Wordy (Imri), were the sons of Hassenaah. We are not given their names except to know whose sons they are. Hassenaah means "thorny"; he is the ancestor of these sons who had returned from exile. Consider, if you will, that the man named Thorny had lived in captivity, and his name expressed his time and circumstances. However, his sons returned from a thorny place to the place God had chosen to dwell among them. They had returned from exile, the thorny area, into the very place where the presence of God dwelt—a place of hope.

Another place in Scripture tells of thorns preceding the presence of God. This time it was not for man to dwell near God but for God to dwell in man. Think of the crown of thorns Jesus wore when He made the way for you to return from your thorny place of captivity into the very presence of God. When Jesus died on the cross, the temple's veil tore in two from top to bottom. It was as though God reached down from heaven with two mighty hands and tore it Himself to make the way for you, me, and every person who chooses to come into His very presence (Mark 15:38).

What is the invitation given in Hebrews 10:19–22? Have you accepted this invitation? Is this easy or difficult for you to do? Why?

While we do not have the names of Hassenaah's sons, the meaning of the Hebrew word for *son* is "build."[vii] Clearly, in context, it means building the family line. However, figuratively and in the context of building the Fish Gate, the root includes: "to build, rebuild, establish, cause to continue."[viii] These sons of Thorny (Hassenaah) were not prickly but working with their brethren, the Israelites, to rebuild the gate, establish a new day in Israel, and cause Israel to continue. Their willingness to build more than their father's name has contributed to our salvation story. Their hope of an earthly kingdom restored set the stage for our eternal hope.

What did these builders build? They built the Fish Gate, most likely named for the fish market nearby or for being the gate through which fish came to market.[ix] Those who build the kingdom of God are called fishers of men (Matthew 4:19). Jesus is the gate through which they bring new believers into God's kingdom (Matthew 7:13). Just like the sons of Hassenaah built an entrance to the city where God's presence dwelt, Jesus's disciples point the way for people to enter His eternal presence. Are you a fisher of people today?

These sons of Hassenaah built the barrier to the city. They put in the beams, doors, locks, and bars. They restored a boundary to block entrance into the city by those who would do it harm, but also a door to open and let in those who sought refuge in God's kingdom. They built the gate. They rebuilt their hope, established a healthy boundary to the city and temple, and helped continue the cause of Israel, their long-awaited Messiah—Jesus. Truly, these were sons and builders of God.

How does Hassenaah's name relate to Nehemiah's time in history? How does it relate to you today?

How does the Fish Gate relate to kingdom building?

What did building the Fish Gate establish for the sons of Hassenaah? How does it relate to us?

Where is God calling you to build in His kingdom today? While times and seasons of life change, being called and equipped to build His kingdom remains a constant. Where have you served in the past? Where are you now, and where do you see yourself building His kingdom in the future?

Read the following scriptures and note how they apply to this section of our study and to your being a child and builder of God:

Matthew 16:17, 18

Matthew 5:9

Luke 20:36

Romans 8:14

Galatians 3:26

How do you respond to these truths?

DAY FOUR

Beyond the sons of Hassenaah, on the western part of the north wall, built Meremoth son of Urijah, son of Koz. He built part of the wall beyond the Fish Gate toward the northwest corner of the wall. His name is a plural name meaning "heights." He is the son of Urijah, which means "flame of Jah."[x] His name suggests a man who is on fire for God. Being named Heights by his father implies his father did so because he was a man on fire for God, or he was prophesying over his son when he named him.

The interesting note here is the name of Heights's (Meremoth's) grandfather, the one who named Heights's father Flame Of Jah (Urijah). Koz translates to a word akin to one we have already heard—"thorn."[xi] Here we see a beautiful progression toward God. The farthest from God was named Thorn. As he turned to look toward God, his son became Flame Of Jah, on fire for God, and his son, in turn, reached Heights they had not known.

It may seem like a stretch, or even a little silly. But if you look at your own life, you may see similarities. First, as a sinner, I was a thorn, prickly and unenjoyable. When I gave my life to Christ, I was on fire for God, heart, mind, and strength (Mark 12:30). As I grow in Christ, I continue to reach new heights and set my children up to rise higher than myself. My life/heart change affects my children's future and their children for generations. Therefore, this is not a stretch; this is a kingdom truth to hold on to and pray over our families as we grow in grace, on fire, and reaching new heights.

What similarities do you see between your history and that of Heights (Meremoth), Flame Of Jah (Urijah), and Thorny (Koz)? Do you see a similar progression in your family? Where are you on this progression?

What does your heart change affect, and for how long?

MESHULLAM

NEHEMIAH 3:4

Heights (Meremoth) was followed on the wall by Meshullam. The only detail we learn about him from Scripture is that he was son of Berechiah and grandson of Meshezabeel. From their names we can learn about their lives in captivity and during the return.

Meshullam means "allied or friend."[xii] His father's name, Berechiah, means "blessing of Jah,"[xiii] and his grandfather's name, Meshezabeel, means "delivered of God."[xiv] In the ancestral names we see a theme. This family processed their situations through faith in the God who is able to bless and deliver, the God who is our friend and ally. When traversing life's ups and downs, we must never forget God is still on the throne.

We can see the contrasting ways men responded to the captivity and return by looking at their ancestral names. How are you traversing your difficulties today? Are you Thorny or Delivered of God? The measure of our character shows through trials. What does your conduct relay to the world about your faith?

I cannot judge. I have my ups and downs. I can be faith-filled, or I can grumble at constantly waiting for the next God-adventure. I can forget to live large in my faith walk, distracted by what has not yet come to fruition. Then I realize why they have not yet materialized: I must grow, and the current trial teaches me where I lack. Therefore, I will be grateful for my trials. I know they will bring me where I want to be, with a character more aligned with God's purposes. I also become more intimate with my Father when I lean on Him through challenging times.

Allied/Friend (Meshullam) repaired beyond the men named Build. In this counterclockwise journey around the wall, we see an undoing of destruction. Similarly, as we build our relationship with Jesus, Satan's destructive plans for our lives are undone, and we increasingly see Jesus as our allied friend. We come to know Him more, and He changes us as we put our faith and trust in Him. Then, because of Jesus's work on the cross, we become allied friends of one another, as we build God's kingdom together for His glory.

How did this family process life's difficulties? How does this compare or contrast to how you deal with them? Give an example.

What must we never forget as we traverse life's ups and downs? How might this affect how we walk through them?

Why can you be grateful in your trials?

How does Jesus become our allied friend, and how do we become His? How have you seen this process work in your own life?

With whom else do we expect to become allied friends? How does this come to fruition? Give an example.

ZADOK
NEHEMIAH 3:4

Beyond Allied/Friend (Meshullam), we turn the corner of the northwest portion of the wall toward the south on the west side and find Zadok son of Baana. Working past Allied/Friend is a man named Just or Righteous (Zadok).[xv] Zadok's father's name, Baana (In Affliction), relates to the wilderness wanderings, when God used affliction to bring about the knowledge of their dependence upon Him (Deuteronomy 8).[xvi] In Affliction's (Baana's) father possibly named him while in exile, remembering the forty years Israel wandered with Moses.

We see a picture in these names of how our affliction led us to repentance, and now we stand justified and righteous through Jesus's shed blood. There exists no other way to be made righteous than to receive the forgiveness Jesus died to give us. Then we commit to follow Him all our days, which His resurrection made possible for us (Romans 5:9, 10).

How are we made righteous?

Tell of a time affliction was used to your benefit.

DAY FIVE

THE TEKOITES

NEHEMIAH 3:5

The Tekoites (Trumpet Blast) repaired to the south of Just/Righteous (Zadok).[xvii] The trumpet blasts of the Old Testament times were critical. They called assemblies together, prepared marches when Israel traversed the wilderness, and called men to war. They were a communication device given by God for the ordering of His children. They were also a terror to Israel's enemies.

I am most excited about two trumpet blasts in Scripture. They refer to experiences with God Himself. Take a look and see if you can tell why I get so excited about them. Record your response.

Exodus 19:19, 20:1

Leviticus 25:9–10

After the heavenly trumpet blast, God spoke audibly to Moses and Israel. They *heard* Him! I love to imagine it. Can you see it in your mind? Think what the atmosphere would have been like. It is exhilarating!

Another of my favorite trumpet blasts is the one used to signal the Jubilee (Leviticus 25:9). The Day of Atonement foreshadowed Jesus's atoning sacrifice on the cross. The trumpet blast of Jubilee signaled Israel's restoration to their inheritance and freedom from all of their debts. It was a reset button on their lives every fifty years. Again, with Jesus we are restored to our destiny. But for us, it is a one-time-for-all-time reset. We do not need to repeat every fifty years because our restoration is final and eternal.

Note what else happened or will happen at the trumpet's blast and your responses.

Joshua 6:5

Matthew 24:31

1 Thessalonians 4:16–17

The individuals known collectively as Trumpet Blast (the Tekoites) have no ancestors listed; their ancestors would also have been Tekoites. Trumpet Blast builds the wall with all the significance of the trumpet blasts of Scripture. They are fulfilling God's call as they return to their city, Jerusalem. They are rebuilding in perilous times under God's protection. They blare out the restorative acts of God through their actions and call out future promises.

How does the Jubilee relate to Jesus and our eternal walk with Him?

Which example of trumpet blasts mentioned speaks most to you? Why?

How does the Tekoites' building of the wall speak a prophetic message?

Are you living in your jubilee; do you know your freedom in Christ? Are you hearing from God personally with the help of the Holy Spirit? Are you letting Him tear down walls in your life meant to keep Him out, and are you allowing Him to build new walls— healthy boundaries—as you grow in Him? Are you looking forward to the day Jesus comes to take you home?

Did you have a "no" answer to any of these questions? Where are you struggling today for your "yes"?

For a no answer, cry out to God. Give Him permission to reveal why and give you direction to help you change your answer to a resounding "YES"! Take time to do it now, then write down the results and even more questions—whatever comes from the time you spend with Him. Then consider sharing it with someone else. What I learn when I choose to be vulnerable with others is that I am not alone. Take a deep breath of courage and share your story. You might be surprised by how many people around you are going through the same experiences. God is good at bringing us to the right groups at perfect times.

Nehemiah and the West Wall

Week Four / Day One

Nehemiah 3:6–12

Nehemiah 3:6

Following Trumpet Blast (the Tekoites), we locate Jehoiada and Meshullam building at the Old Gate. Jehoiada (Jah Known or Jah Knows) is the son of Paseah (Limping).[i] Meshullam (Allied/Friend) is the son of Besodeiah (In the Counsel of Jah, With the Counsel of Jah, or In the Secret of the Lord).[ii] The Old Gate was probably so named because of its age. It had been around a long time, most likely being one of the original gates to the city.

We continue to see the redemptive story written into the building of Nehemiah's wall. The man named Jah Knows/Known (Jehoiada) built alongside Allied/Friend (Meshullam). He is born of a man called Limping (Paseah), and Jah Knows/Known is the one who set the beams, doors, locks, and bars. We continue to see the progression from one who comes from a lame, broken history to Jah knows—He sees.

Not only does God see our broken places but He knows how to heal. He alone knows how to deliver us to our new state called Known by Him, no longer left to scratch out a living in a dark world but able to see His glorious light. We are not merely known by Him; we know and receive Him in our hearts, and we are made new (2 Corinthians 3:18).

What a glorious promise and journey we have before us. How do we get there? We enter through the old-gate-made-new and build alongside our Allied Friend, Jesus. He is the door and the way. The Old Gate transforms as the Old Testament transitions to the New and the way made by Jesus's shed blood. A new door opened to us as the veil tore in two (Matthew 7:13, 14; 27:51; John 14:6).

Allied/Friend (Meshullam) is the son of With the Counsel of the Lord or In the Secret Of the Lord (Besodeiah). We must heed the counsel of our allied friend, Jesus, to build alongside Him.

What more do you learn about the secret place from Matthew 6:6?

One who builds well will spend much time in the secret place with the Lord. How does one find one's way into the secret place, according to Luke 10:22? How does the intimacy of this make you feel? How do you want to respond to this truth?

Jah Known (Jehoiada) and Allied/Friend (Meshullam) built and made the Old Gate new. They laid the beams, doors, locks, and bars to ensure the safety of those who made it through the gate to God's kingdom. They could lock out the adversaries who warred against their souls. Like the Old Gate made new, the Old Testament makes way for the New Testament. The old points to the new.

What do you learn about the old and new from Galatians 3:24?

The old gate led to the same place as the new gate, but the journey changed. The old gate is associated with David and the Law.

How does David relate here, according to 2 Samuel 5:6, 7?

The old gate led into the place of the conquering king and the old worship system, where men had to conquer their sins by works of sacrifices and offerings. It proved humankind's inability to save themselves and their need for a savior.

Do you know the safety of living on the other side of this gate, whose beams, doors, locks, and bars are sure? How does this look in your life?

Read Romans 8:1. What does it say about those who are in Christ?

Do you know, believe, and walk in this truth? I hope you know this ultimate freedom and safety in Christ. If you do not, ask a leader in your church for counsel to help you walk through the gate and know your security behind the gate.

Read the following scriptures and note what you learn about the intimacy of the secret place. How do you respond to these scriptures? Do you feel you fall short of these, or do they encourage you and invite you into a deeper relationship with Jesus?
John 10:14

1 Corinthians 8:3

John 15:9–11

How do we see a redemptive story in Jehoiada's and Meshullam's working side by side?

How does the Old Gate relate to Jesus and redemption?

What does one who builds well spend time doing?

How has this section encouraged or challenged you?

This is a good time for another testimony. If you are studying in a group, have someone new share their salvation story. If you are doing this study independently, write a testimony of God's goodness in your life and ask Him to bring an opportunity this week to share.

DAY TWO

MELATIAH, JADON, AND THE MEN OF GIBEON AND MIZPAH: THE GOVERNOR'S RESIDENCE
NEHEMIAH 3:7

This was quite a group working together. We begin with Melatiah (Jah Has Delivered).[iii] He is not merely living in hope but walking in faith, knowing what has already been. How are you walking out your faith experience? Do you walk as one who is delivered, or are you still walking as though there has been no change?

What does Paul teach us in 2 Corinthians 5:7 and Romans 6:5–6?

You are delivered; does your life proclaim this truth? If not, why not? What will you do about it today?

Following Jah Has Delivered (Melatiah), Jadon the Meronothite repaired. His name translates as "thankful," with a root word meaning "to revere or worship."[iv] Meronothite means "joyful shouter."[v] In this place, we have a man building with and beside a man named Jah Has Delivered. This man is Thankful, rooted in reverent worship, and coming from a place of Joyful Shouting.

Do you see the beautiful progression? We are delivered; the old is made new. What else can we do but be thankful in reverent worship, unable to contain our joyful shouts of praise to our loving Father? We can find no better place to be than when we understand what God has done for us—so much so it elicits joyful shouts of praise and worship from the depths of our souls. Do you know what He has done for you? Shout for joy!

The men of Gibeon built along with Deliverance (Melatiah—Jah Had Delivered), Thankfulness (Jadon—Thankful), and Joyful Shouting (Meronothite—Joyful Shouter). Read Joshua 9:1–21 and note what you learn about the Gibeonites.

The Gibeonites had remained and assimilated into Israel. Their city name means "hill city." It was a Levitical city inside the territory of Benjamin (Son of the Right Hand).[vi] It is interesting to note that Benjamin's territory was alongside Judah's. Judah carried the kings' line and held the Law and temple. Judah protected the judicial and religious branches of Israel. Therefore, Judah protected the Son of the Right Hand, Jesus, who entered the line of the kings of Israel through adoption.

Where was Jesus seated when He ascended back to the Father? (See Ephesians 1:20; Hebrews 8:1)

As a Levitical city, Hill City (Gibeon) speaks to those who carry the Word of the Lord. The Levites carried the Law physically. Where is the law written now, according to Jeremiah 31:31–33?

What did Jesus say to His disciples in Matthew 5:14–16? How can this be applied to the Gibeonites and their city? How can you apply it to yourself today?

This group of builders provides a lesson in Christian living. We are delivered, thankful in reverence, and we worship with joyful shouts of praise. We have become a part of God's family, grafted in, and we cannot be silent and hide our transformation. We must let our lights shine in this dark world so others might become as we are: delivered, thankful, worshipers of God.

Finally, this group of builders and examples of Christian living finished with the men of Mizpah. What else could there be in our list of Christian-living attributes? We seem to have it covered, don't we? We have deliverance, gratitude, worship, and evangelism. What could be missing? Well, Mizpah translates to "Watchtower."[vii]

A watchtower was where a guard stood to watch for enemies approaching the city or fortress. Watchmen remained alert and continually scanned the horizon for threats. They did not take their job lightly because they were the first line of defense, sounding the warning to awaken others to impending dangers. Their job was intended to protect themselves and others.

Before we can be a watchman on the wall, what must we do, according to Matthew 26:41? Why? Share an example of how this might look today.

We must be watchful in prayer and submit to God's Word so we do not fall prey to the old man and become tempted into sin (Romans 6:6; Ephesians 4:22; Colossians 3:9).

Read 1 Thessalonians 5:5–8. What do you learn about being watchful from these verses? In what way(s) are you challenged or encouraged?

What more is required for being watchful, according to Ephesians 6:13? How can you apply this?

According to Philippians 2:12, what must you do before you can come alongside someone else to help them?

Paul wrote about taking up the armor of God in his letter to the Ephesians. Paul's message tells us we possess all the tools necessary to guard our hearts against evil, the wiles of our enemy, and our flesh. The necessity of the watchman is for us to continue on toward our salvation. First we must watch and pray, to work out our salvation, and then we can be of service to come alongside others as they work out theirs.

Interestingly, this group of builders repaired the Governor's Residence, also known as the Throne of the Governor. It was not merely where the governor lived but also where he dispensed justice and judgment.[viii] What a beautiful theme for repairing the area of justice and judgment—having been brought about by Jah's deliverance through shouts of joy born of reverent gratitude, which shines the light of Christ. The importance of watching oneself with sober judgment comes to light as we understand the final judgment to come. We will one day give an account of how we spent our life here. Justice will prevail. If we enter this throne room covered by the blood of Jesus, we will inherit eternal life. If we enter without conversion, we will undoubtedly receive our judgment and doom.

Before Nehemiah returned, an outsider appointed by Persia's conquering king had filled the position of governor. After Nehemiah, people from the region occupied the Throne of the Governor. Do you see? Before Christ, we were ruled by sin and by the imposter, Satan. However, when we come into the freedom boundaries of Christ, Satan and his outsiders no longer have legal access. Our Friend, who has made the way for our justification, occupies the throne of government and judgment (Romans 3:24, 5:1; Galatians 2:16, 17; 3:24; 5:4). The rightful King enthroned in heaven and in our hearts reigns supreme. Praise His Holy Name!

What should elicit joyful shouts of praise and worship from our lips?

Where do we carry God's Word? How should that affect the way we engage the world?

How is this group a lesson in Christian living?

What must we do to become watchmen, and what is our armor? In what ways are we equipped, according to Paul?

Why is sober judgment toward self so important?

What are the benefits of the freedom boundaries of Christ?

DAY THREE

UZZIEL AND HANANIAH: AS FAR AS THE BROAD WALL

NEHEMIAH 3:8

Moving toward the Broad Wall, building beside the Governor's Residence, is Uzziel (Strength of God or My Strength Is God).[ix] He is the son of a goldsmith, which means he, too, is a goldsmith. How wonderful for him to follow the men of the last section who exemplified the code of Christian living. We genuinely do find our strength is in God. His father is Harhaiah (Fearing Jah).[x]

Read the following verses and note what you learn about fearing God from the writer of Ecclesiastes.

Ecclesiastes 8:12

Ecclesiastes 12:13

What did Abraham learn about fearing God, and what were the results? (See Genesis 22:1–14.)

Abraham learned this truth when he obeyed God and took his son Isaac as an offering to God. God stopped him before he could follow through and provided Abraham with a ram for the sacrifice. For Abraham, fear of God preceded provision and blessing.

My Strength Is God (Uzziel) was born of Fearing Jah (Harhaiah). No better way exists for God to be our strength. It must be born of our reverent fear, which lifts God to the highest place and bows our faces to the ground in humble adoration. Moses and the Israelites sang this line after passing through the Red Sea: "The Lord is my strength and song, and He has become my salvation; He is my God, and I will praise Him; my father's God and I will exalt Him" (Exodus 15:2 NKJV). The goldsmith exalted God by humbling himself to build the wall when it was not his expertise. He did what was in front of him to do in or to build the kingdom.

His name is My Strength Is God, but his profession speaks of a mild persona. One does not picture a goldsmith as a man of strength but more as a man of artistry, maybe adorned with gold. However, a goldsmith is also a jeweler. Jewels speak of riches and majesty. Jewels were found in royal courts, embedded in royal crowns, and worn as symbols of wealth and honor. Jewels refract light. As the light enters the gemstone's surface, it changes speed and direction. It slows, and as it changes direction and returns to the surface, it disperses colors.

What does God say of His people in the following verses? What benefits do you see? Zechariah 9:16

Malachi 3:17

Jesus is the Light of the world. As we receive Him as Lord and Savior and invite Him to come into our hearts, we receive His light. When it enters us, it slows to do its work. When it comes back out of us at a different angle, it diffuses His light and colors. It changes our experience with the world and the world's with us. Let your light so shine (Matthew 5:14–16)!

The perfumer, Hananiah (Jah Has Favored), worked alongside Uzziel (My Strength Is God).[xi] To have Jah's favor means to have Him turn His eyes toward you. His intentions toward you are for good and not for evil (Jeremiah 29:11). "For the eyes of the LORD run to and fro throughout the whole earth, to show Himself strong on behalf of those whose heart is loyal to Him" (2 Chronicles 16:9a NKJV). As a perfumer, Hananiah (Jah Has Favored) would most likely carry a fragrance about him.

I cannot help but connect the Lord's favor with the Lord's fragrance. Jah Has Favored (Hananiah) most likely carried a fragrance upon him from working with perfumes. When the eyes of the Lord are upon us (when we carry His favor), we, too, have His fragrance about us.

Read 2 Corinthians 2:14–15 and note what it says about the fragrance of Christ. How do you see this in the world? How do you see this in your life?

I have smelled the fragrance of the Lord on a few occasions. One of those times was when I was meeting with a few ladies at a local restaurant in the community. We noticed a scent and thought someone had used an air freshener or cleanser. We asked the waitress, and she said they had not. Then she smelled it, too! We realized it was the fragrance of the Lord and were able to testify to her of Jesus. In the following weeks, she would come to us and talk about church and Sunday school and even sing us some of the Sunday School songs she remembered from when she used to go to church. It was a very precious time.

Another time I smelled the fragrance of the Lord was on a Sunday morning just before I was to preach. I was battling anxiety because I could not outline my sermon or develop my points. I just knew the gist of it and the scriptures to use. It was way outside of my preaching/teaching box and comfort zone. I was staring out through the dining room window, looking over my backyard, trying to pray and get a grip on myself, when the most beautiful fragrance suddenly embraced me. I knew the Lord was telling me He would come through for me in such a way I could not doubt Him. So I relaxed and preached an excellent sermon—like I had notes, an outline, and points!

On one final occasion, I went out of town with a few friends to seek the Lord together. I have a small vial of anointing oil, and I had filled it with olive oil from my kitchen cupboard. The Lord met with us in powerful ways; at one point we anointed each other with the oil. Someone mentioned how good it smelled, and I corrected them, saying it was merely kitchen olive oil. Then we all smelled it, and it was abundantly fragrant. That was nearly ten years ago, and the same oil is in the vial. It still carries a fragrance not its own, and it has not gone rancid or run out. It is the favor of the Lord, and it is beautiful.

Here we have, building on the wall, a man named Jah Has Favored (Hananiah), who carries His fragrance. This beautiful aroma will permeate the physical wall and the spiritual kingdom they build. It is a foreshadowing of the heavenly kingdom to come. Wherever you go, may you carry the fragrance of knowing Him, and may the fragrance linger long after you have left. May you permeate every area with a saving knowledge of Jesus.

How do we find strength in God?

What does fear of God precede?

How are God's people like jewels?

What does it mean to have Jah's favor?

In what ways and places do you diffuse the fragrance of the Lord?

DAYS FOUR AND FIVE

REPHAIAH, JEDAIAH, AND HATTUSH: THE BROAD WALL
NEHEMIAH 3:9, 10

The Broad Wall's name came from—you guessed it—its size. It extended from the Gate of Ephraim, not mentioned in these Nehemiah verses, to the Tower of the Furnaces. It was broader (even double-walled) than other sections of the wall. Joash, an Israelite king, tore the wall down during the conflicts of the divided kingdom (2 Chronicles 25:23). King Uzziah is credited with this rebuild after Joash's destructive forces had toppled it (2 Chronicles 26:9). When the Chaldeans conquered Jerusalem, they were unable to destroy the rebuilt wall, due to its strength.[xii]

Scripture names three men as workers on the Broad Wall: Rephaiah, Jedaiah, and Hattush. The first man named, following the jewelers and perfumers, was Jah Has Cured (Rephaiah).[xiii] He is the son of Hur (White Linen),[xiv] and he is reported to have been the ruler of half of Jerusalem. While his name means "white linen," the root meaning is "being or becoming free," such as from a crevice, a serpent, or a prison cell.[xv] Sounds biblical.

Read Romans 6:18, 22–23. How does this parallel White Linen (Hur)? What are the blessings and expectations?

This man, White Linen (Hur), fathered a son and named him Jah Has Cured. What a beautiful picture of our salvation in Christ. We are set free from a serpent's crevice, from our jail of sin and death, and we have received the cure only Jah could bring to make us righteous in Christ (Romans 5:19).

What does Revelation 3:5 promise to the one who overcomes? How does that speak to you today?

Beyond Jah Has Cured (Rephaiah) toiled Praised Of Jah (Jedaiah) son of Snubnosed (Harumaph).[xvi] "Snubnosed" could very well be a comment on physical appearance, though for a name given at birth, this is curious. If we look at the name's root, we uncover meanings such as "banning, prohibiting, or setting aside for destruction."[xvii] The root for *nose* can mean "nose or countenance."[xviii] If we look at these, we can see a man whose face is set toward destruction, as the wall very much was when he was born to the name. However, we see God's redemptive purposes for the wall, Jerusalem, and humanity in the birth of Snubnosed's (Harumaph's) son, Praised Of Jah (Jedaiah).

History turns away from what was set for destruction and prohibited to what elicits the very pleasure of God. We see in the name one who confesses the name of God and gives thanks and praise to God with hands extended in reverent worship. We turn from an angry and destructive countenance to a face turned upward in total joy and surrender to the One who supplies all our needs. In this posture, we observe the one empowered and equipped by God to build His kingdom.

Hattush means "assembled," and he is the son of Hashabniah (Thought of Jah).[xix] He repaired beside Praised Of Jah (Jedaiah) and Jah Has Cured (Rephaiah). What a wonderful place to find oneself. Is this not a picture of the Church? We are the assembled. We lift our praises to God, our hands lifted high. He heals us and changes our countenance, and we proclaim His glorious name. He equips us for the joy of building His kingdom. The enemy will never penetrate His broad wall; His is a sure salvation. We are safe. We shall continue to assemble as thoughts of Jah draw us to this assembly.

Write out Revelation 22:17.

Read Hebrews 10:24–25. Why is it essential for us to assemble with other believers?

What are we set free of through salvation in Christ? How are we cured, and what are we given to wear?

How does our countenance change when we come to Christ?

How are we empowered through our new life in Christ? What are we able to do?

What do you glean from the notes on Hattush? How are you challenged or inspired?

MALCHIJAH AND HASHUB: TOWER OF THE FURNACES/OVENS

NEHEMIAH 3:11

Next on the wall are Malchijah and Hashub. They worked on repairing the Tower of the Furnaces. They are located on the western wall just north of the Valley Gate, where Nehemiah entered and exited the city the night he surveyed the wall.

Malchijah means "king of Jah, appointed by Jah, or my king is Jah."[xx] One truth is sure: one cannot be appointed or positioned in the Lord unless one makes Him their king. I would venture to say all three ring true of the man, as these translations hold a communal point. He was named for a time in history characterized by a return to hope in and surrender to God Most High.

My King Is Jah (Malchijah) was born to another man whose name meant "snubnosed" (Harim).[xxi] Since we just discussed this, we will not venture into detail again here. We have seen the transition of a man with a face set against; then, by the power and activity of God in his life, he bows down and raises his voice to proclaim his son as My King Is Jah (Malchijah). It is a beautiful transition from despair into an assurance of hope; this is where the hearts of the men and women of Jerusalem are as they build the wall.

Hashub built with My King Is Jah (Malchijah) on the Tower of the Furnaces. His name means "intelligent."[xxii] He was the son of Pahath-Moab, which means "pit of Moab."[xxiii] A history lesson on Moab makes one suspect the name as akin to a curse. Moab was the product of an incestuous relationship by Lot, Abraham's nephew (Genesis 19:30–37). The country of Moab was a neighbor to Israel and an enemy of the same. To say one's name meant the "pit of Moab" could possibly describe the condition of living in the time of captivity. We can't know for certain, of course, since neither Scripture nor the definition is clear on this point. Instead, we will leave it as an interesting observation. We know the man named Pit Of Moab (Pahath-Moab) named his son Intelligent (Hashub). What may have begun in despair would end with eyes turned toward God, from whom his help would come. Help came to Israel through Ezra and Nehemiah, who led the restoration of worship and boundaries in Jerusalem. True intelligence begins within a faith relationship with God (Proverbs 1:7; 9:10).

As stated, the Tower of the Furnaces sat north of the Valley Gate. As a tower, it would be a defensible position. The name also suggests it is where chefs prepared meals for the kings of Judah and all whom they would entertain. They would also supply the market with the same.

The tower was the hearth of Jerusalem, where the fires burned and chefs prepared sustenance. Jerusalem housed the center of worship—the temple. We are, in Christ, the temple of the Holy Spirit, and the Holy Spirit's symbol is a flame or fire. He is the hearth of our being. He inspires and ignites a holy passion in us to pursue righteousness, feast on God's Word, and share the life-giving sustenance of life in Christ with those around us. God appoints us to use spiritual intelligence to meet the spiritual and physical needs of the world around us. Will you ask the Holy Spirit to ignite a fire in you today?

How does one become appointed or positioned in the Lord?

Share a time when you transitioned from despair to assurance of hope.

Where does true intelligence begin?

How is the Holy Spirit akin to the hearth of Jerusalem?

Have you given Holy Spirit permission to ignite His fire inside of you? What does that look like in your life?

SHALLUM AND DAUGHTERS:

BETWEEN THE TOWER OF THE FURNACES AND THE VALLEY GATE

NEHEMIAH 3:12

Shallum and his daughters worked between the Tower of the Furnaces and the Valley Gate. Shallum's name means "retribution."[xxiv] He was a son of Halohesh (Enchanter or Whisperer).[xxv] Retribution (Shallum), according to Nehemiah 3:12, was the leader of half the district of Jerusalem. Retribution, at its root, is "requital." A synonym for these words is "vengeance." Retribution's (Shallum's) name might reflect a desire to see God's vengeance on Israel's enemies; God said, "Vengeance is mine" (Deuteronomy 32:35). It might also lean toward this enchanter coming to terms with a Holy God's just retribution for the willful sins of His children. Maybe he had come to terms with this appropriate requital (compensation).

The name Enchanter or Whisperer—as in to mumble a spell—(Halohesh) gives a clue to where this man's father was when he named him. Israel and Judah did not remove the soothsayers, which was part of the reason for the captivity (Isaiah 2:6). This name might be a statement of the times they were in and the bent of their exiled ancestors.

Read Deuteronomy 30:1–10. What was God's purpose for Israel and Judah in captivity and exile? What was the intended outcome? Can you tell of a time when you experienced a similar motivator?

Read Hebrews 7:25. What is Jesus able to do for us? Why?

What is beautiful about the Lord is His ability to turn retribution into restoration. He did not send Israel and Judah into captivity to eradicate them but to turn their hearts back to Him (Deuteronomy 30:3). What is most important for any of us to do amid trials and storms, whether of our own making or not, is to cry out to our God, who is able to deliver us to the uttermost (Hebrews 7:25). We must believe He is who He says He is, fall on our knees in surrender of our will for His perfect will, and make Him Lord of our lives.

We read that Retribution (Shallum) built on the wall with his daughters. We are given no more information about them. What is displayed clearly in the text is that women were welcome to assist in kingdom building/repairing. They were invited and released to work alongside the men in the work God had assigned them. Like *son*, the root of *daughter* is "to build," as in to build a family. God's sons and daughters are builders of His kingdom, both genders rooted in the words and idea of "to build."

God does not make mistakes; He is perfect and intentional. You are not only invited but also equipped to build the kingdom. Embrace your calling. Where did the builders work? They built where they lived, right at their homes or businesses. They did not have special training as builders. They were farmers, shepherds, bakers, jewelers, perfumers, priests, sons, and daughters. They built Nehemiah's wall in just fifty-two days—record time—when they came together for a single purpose. God can do mighty acts wherever His people work in unity.

Why did God send Israel and Judah into captivity?

What must you do when you find yourself in trials and storms? What if the trial is of your own making?

What do we learn women were welcome to do in kingdom building? What does it look like today? What should it look like today?

Where did they build? How are you applying this to your life?

What happened when the people of God came together for a single purpose?

Nehemiah and the South Wall

Nehemiah 3:13–22

HANUN AND INHABITANTS OF ZANOAH: THE VALLEY GATE

NEHEMIAH 3:13

Past Retribution (Shallum) and his building daughters, built Hanun and the inhabitants of Zanoah working at the Valley Gate. Hanun's name means "favored."[i] At its root, his name means "to bend or stoop in kindness to an inferior."[ii] However, it has a further rooted connotation: "to seek favor bestowed upon."[iii] Zanoah, the place they were from, means "rejected or cast off."[iv] Building at the Valley Gate, through which Nehemiah had first exited and entered the city to view the wall, were located those Rejected or Cast Off (Zanoans) building alongside the one named Favored (Hanun).

Isn't this just like the Lord? He, Jesus, is truly the Favored One. Those who accept Him as Lord and Savior join Him in building His kingdom. We were rejected and cast off, but when we work alongside the Favored One, our rejection turns to favor and acceptance (Ephesians 2:13; Hebrews 7:25). It is one of many beautiful dichotomies in God's kingdom.

The Valley Gate is between the Tower of the Furnaces and the Dung/Refuse Gate on the city's west side.[v] As you can see on the map of the wall in the appendix, there is a vast distance between the tower and the gate. One thousand cubits separate them, and Favored and Rejected worked together to build this wall section.

Who do we locate building alongside those rejected and cast off? How can you apply this to kingdom service today?

What can you take away from this example for ministry and service in your spheres of influence?

How might it change your perspective on what qualifies someone to work alongside you?

How might it qualify you to work alongside someone when you feel inadequate?

We all have a place, purpose, and destiny in God's kingdom. When we surrender our will for His, we gain full access to the future designed for us (Ephesians 2:10). We cannot destroy God's destiny plan. We can walk away, but it will be there waiting for us when we return because He remains faithful.

What challenges do you face in seeking God's will for your life today? What challenges keep you from living your full potential for God? Knowing He designed you for His plan, will you seek to humble yourself before Him in faith? What can you do this week, or even now, to begin meeting your destiny, call, and purpose?

MALCHIAH: DUNG GATE
NEHEMIAH 3:14

At the southern end of the wall, just before turning north along the eastern side, following Favored (Hanun) and Rejected (inhabitants of Zanoah), we observe Malchiah son of Rechab, ruler of part of Beth Haccerem, building at the Dung or Refuse Gate. Malchiah's name means "king of/appointed by Jah" or "my king is Jah."[vi] He is the son of Rechab, which is a primitive root meaning "to ride or to dispatch, to set upon, whether animal or vehicle, such as a chariot: rider."[vii]

Here we see the man whose name is My King Is Jah or King Of Jah (Malchiah), son of one whose name suggests much travel, whether due to dispatch or exile. We see one proclaiming his God in his son's name, My King Is Jah; Jah, the God of heaven and highest glory and power. We hear his father's rejoicing in naming his son as exiles began to return home after the extended displacement. He saw a miracle he could not fathom and gave his son a name to reflect the glory of God for all to hear.

We learn from this verse that Appointed by/King Of Jah (Malchiah) was the ruler of part of Beth Haccerem, or house of the vineyard, a place in Judah.[viii] This man who ruled in a place named for a lovely vineyard, built in a most unlovely area: the Dung or Refuse Gate. As discussed in Chapter two, this gate stood above the refuse dump. Only a man who truly knows his king is Jah could properly humble himself to work in such an undesirable location.

Can you relate to this? Where are you willing to go for Him now, where you would never have considered going before? Even more so, whom would you serve since being transformed by your King?

I remember meeting a homeless man in Anchorage, Alaska. We were following him to provide him with a bag of food. Looking back, it was both humorous and dangerous. In a town we were not from, we were intentionally stalking a homeless man—with good intentions. It was a God moment. When he let us catch him, we realized we had followed him into a vacant parking garage. The man said he had purposefully led us there—gulp. Then he gratefully received our gifts and told us his tragic story.

Sadly, this man thought he was living the life he deserved. He believed he was living God's punishment for his life. My heart broke as I spoke value and love into his life. By the end of our conversation, the man who had tried to outrun us took me in his arms and gave me the most beautiful hug I have ever received. Tears well in my eyes as I write this, remembering when he pressed his cheek against mine. I felt so honored.

I did not see a man who was unclean or possibly dangerous. Instead, I saw a child of God in great pain. It has been over a decade, and I will never forget him. I continue to pray for him. With the deepest longing, I pray he will one day read these words for himself, knowing our encounter was not random but appointed by Jah.

What did it take for Appointed by Jah/King Of Jah (Malchiah) to work in this area? What would it take for you to work in a similar place?

Have you changed your mind about things you used to consider refuse? Where or to whom are you willing to go for Him now, that you would not have considered before?

Share a time when you served in an unlikely place for Jesus.

Write the following scriptures:

Matthew 5:16

Ephesians 2:10

Take a minute to search your heart and mind. Invite God to reveal any area where you still view any place, person, or group as undesirable (a dung heap). Then take a moment and ask Him where He would have you shine His light this week, knowing He has already prepared the good work in you. Write what comes to mind below.

Day Two

SHALLUN: THE FOUNTAIN GATE, THE WALL OF THE POOL OF SHILOAH, THE KING'S GARDEN, AND THE STAIRS FROM THE CITY OF DAVID

NEHEMIAH 3:15

We are rounding the wall's southern section and heading up the east side back toward where it all began. We discover Shallun, ruler of part of Mizpah and son of Colhozeh, building at the Fountain Gate, the wall of the Pool of Shiloah, the King's Garden, and the stairs to and from the City of David. Though it sounds like a lot, these four wall sections covered a smaller area than the sites suggest. The extent of repairs required most likely determined the amount of wall covered. That suggests that the section between the Valley and Dung Gates did not need as much repair. It could explain why that group was able to cover a more significant area than this group. It could also indicate one group had more people to do the work. However, looking at the map, we see the sections Shallun worked on were very close together and did not cover as much of the wall as it sounds.

Shallun, like Shallum, means "retribution."[ix] His father's name was Colhozeh, meaning "every seer or all-seeing."[x] The meaning of Shallun, "retribution," at its root word suggests one who is purchasable for a fee or bribable.[xi] His father, All-Seeing (Colhozeh), named him Retribution rooted in purchasable. Since we are in a restructuring portion of scripture, may I suggest he is building in the right place at the right time?

The Fountain Gate translates as "eye, such as an eye of the landscape."[xii] This builder's father's name, All-Seeing (Colhozeh), does not escape our attention. Retribution (Shallun), builds at the Eye (Fountain Gate), repairing or restoring the gate. Can you imagine your All-Seeing Father in heaven, whose eyes are upon you, also knows precisely how to restore you?

Isn't it interesting that the author chose this moment to detail the restoration? Our God is in every detail of our lives, restoring us to the destiny He created for us. Here, in this place, is where Retribution (Shallun) built and repaired. Specifically, "he built it, covered it, hung its doors with its bolts and bars" (Nehemiah 3:15).

"He built it": God created you. What does Psalms 139:13–15 say about God's creating you?

"He covered it": You are covered—by the blood of Jesus, who paid the ransom. Look up the following scriptures and note what you learn about Jesus's covering you.
Romans 3:24–25

1 Timothy 2:3–6

 His name was Retribution, rooted with the negative connotation of one corruptible and willing to take a bribe. However, no bribe can pay for salvation. The cost of sin is blood, and Jesus paid it all.

"He hung the doors": God set you in a place and time chosen from the beginning of time. What does Psalms 139:16 say about this?

"With bolts and bars": He set us in place and secured our place with His blood. Look at Hebrews 7:25–27 and note how and why He can secure you.

We can only respond with words like these: to Him be all glory, honor, and praise. Write out Jude 1:25, then take a moment to thank God for all He has done for you.

How do you respond to the correlations of "built it," "covered it," "hung the doors," and "bolts and bars"? Does this change your perspective in any way? Do you feel secure in the Lord today? Why or why not?

Retribution (Shallun) then repaired the place of the Pool of Shiloah and the steps going up to the City of David. We discussed this pool in chapter two; it was also known as the Virgin's Well and was where Jesus sent a man for healing. The virgin Mary bore Jesus, the babe and child King, our Savior.

As Retribution (Shallun) and the rest repair the city wall, their acts cry out a prophetic message of the salvation of the Lord that is to come—and has come to us. This pool is where healing takes place. "You were washed, . . . you were sanctified, . . . you were justified in the name of the Lord Jesus and by the Spirit of our God" (1 Corinthians 6:11).

Finally, the King's Garden, or the enclosure or hedge about the garden, was Retribution's (Shallun's) final place of repair.[xiii] He has been ransomed and washed, and the hedging in is about to begin. Only one place in Scripture explicitly speaks of a hedge as divine protection around one of God's children.

Read Job 1:10 and note what you learn about God's hedge of protection.

I am sure you will agree with me; this is the kind of hedge I want Satan to see around my life. What encouragement do you receive from Romans 8:38, 39?

What about you? Are you living life within the hedge of God's protection? Too many Christians today are living a compromised and complacent life. He has created you, died to save you, and restored you to your destiny if you have placed your faith in Him. Are you living your life today as though all of this is true, or are you just living like you have a one-way ticket out of hell? God has made you on purpose for a purpose and has undoubtedly placed His purpose within your heart.

Will you ask Him to check your hedges today for any places you have left unattended? If He points areas out to you, will you allow Him to help you get back on track to dream a dream only He can fulfill? Will you choose faith, believing He created you to fulfill your destiny, even if it seems too big? It is too big, so you will have to rely on Him, because He wants to do life with you. Consider these questions and write a prayer to Jesus today.

This verse says Retribution (Shallun) repaired as far as the stairs. What interests me is that they are said to lead down from the City of David, as though they are an exit, not an entrance. Why wouldn't the text say, "the stairs going up to the City of David?" Possibly because this is not a main entrance into the city. It is near the King's Garden and the House of the Mighty and may have been solely for the king and his armies. As a thoroughfare, it may have been off limits. I can find nothing to confirm this theory. But we can glean that after being restored to our destiny, we become sent ones. Our focus turns from getting in ourselves to showing others the way in.

Why would God give you a destiny too big for you?

What do you dream of doing? How does that dream benefit kingdom building?

DAY THREE

NEHEMIAH: TOMBS OF DAVID, MAN-MADE POOL, AS FAR AS THE HOUSE OF THE MIGHTY
NEHEMIAH 3:16

Beyond the stairs, we locate Nehemiah son of Abuk building and repairing the tombs of David, the man-made pool, and the House of the Mighty. No, this is not our Nehemiah from Persia. This Nehemiah ruled half the district of Beth Zur (House of the Rock).[xiv]

Nehemiah's name means "consolation of Jah" or "Jah comforts."[xv] His father's name, Abuk, means "strong devastation or stern depopulator."[xvi] I think we get the idea. His father received his name during a dreadful time. In the exile, Jerusalem and Judah were quickly depopulated. But we see here, initially with Cyrus's decree and then with this rebuilding of Jerusalem's wall, the consolation of Jah; we see God's comfort in action (2 Chronicles 36:22, 23).

What did Jesus say about Peter's confession of faith? (Matthew 16:18)

What do you learn about Jesus from the following verses?
1 Corinthians 3:9–11

1 Corinthians 10:4

Hebrews 6:1

This man, Consolation Of Jah (Nehemiah), from House of the Rock (Beth Zur), was entrusted to repair and rebuild the tombs of David and other earthly kings. Here, laid to rest, were David and all the kings who succeeded him to Hezekiah. The consolation of Jah is knowing we do not serve an earthly king who remains entombed. Instead, we serve a Savior King who defeated death and the grave and rose again to life (Mark 16:6; Revelation 1:5)!

Consolation of Jah (Nehemiah) did not stop at the tombs of David. He continued to rebuild and repair the man-made pool. Commentators seem to agree this is the pool made by Hezekiah during the siege by Sennacherib (2 Chronicles 32:4).[xvii] It was a life-sustaining water source within the wall, purposed to get them through tough times.

A river of God flows from the throne of God (Revelation 22:1). Hezekiah's pool was a life-sustaining force within the city's walls. You, too, have a life-sustaining river of water flowing through you as a Christ follower.

John 7:38. What is the result for the one who believes in Jesus?

According to Acts 1:5, how is this made possible?

Finally, we see Consolation of Jah (Nehemiah) repairing the House of the Mighty. This title certainly brings to mind David's mighty men (2 Samuel 23:8–39). It is most likely where these men and other soldiers stayed when on watch or getting battle-ready. The consolation of Jah is His ability to make us all mighty warriors in Christ.

Since we have received the Holy Spirit as believers, the weapons of our warfare have changed. Look up 2 Corinthians 10:3–6 and note the truths of warfare found there.

We also have a change in our armor. Note what Ephesians 6:10–18 tells you about your spiritual armor.

What is the consolation of Jah at the House of the Mighty?

How have your armor and weapons of warfare changed? How do you employ them? Where and how often do you use them?

DAY FOUR

LEVITES AND REHUM: FROM THE HOUSE OF THE MIGHTY TO THE ASCENT TO THE ARMORY
NEHEMIAH 3:17

Following Consolation of Jah (Nehemiah), we come to a string of names along the wall that are not associated with a location. They are repairing between the House of the Mighty and the Ascent to the Armory. Here we notice Levites, the descendants of Jacob and Leah's third-born son, Levi. Leah named him Joined To (Levi) because she believed he would cause her husband to be joined to her (Genesis 29:34).[xviii] His descendants were the priests in Israel. They were mediators between God and man—joining them, if you will.

Joined To (the Levites) served under Rehum, son of Bani. Rehum's name means "compassionate," and his father's means "built."[xix] Therefore, Consolation Of Jah (Nehemiah), Joined To (Levites), and Compassion (Rehum) built between the House of the Mighty and the Ascent to the Armory. I think you can see and feel the connection if you are in Christ. Consolation of Jah, joined to compassion, builds an armory. We are never more secure than when we are found in (joined to) Christ (1 Corinthians 6:17, 19).

Where are we found to be most secure? How do you see this in your life?

What do the following verses say about being in Christ? (Personalize your answers with "I" statements.)
Romans 3:24

Romans 6:11

Romans 6:23

Romans 8:1, 2

Romans 8:39

Ephesians 2:6

Ephesians 2:7

We could look up many more scriptures, but are these not soul-affirming? How do you respond to these truths today? Write your thoughts/responses below.

HASHABIAH
NEHEMIAH 3:17

Hashabiah falls in line behind Consolation Of Jah (Nehemiah), Joined To (the Levites), and Compassion (Rehum). His name means "Jah has regarded."[xx] Keilah means "citadel or fortress."[xxi] A citadel is a city's core fortress. As noted previously, Jesus is our fortress and safe place if we remain in Him (John 15:1–6).

What does Jesus do when we fall into unfaithfulness, according to 2 Timothy 2:13? Why?

THEIR BRETHREN AND BAVAI OF KEILAH
NEHEMIAH 3:18

Between Jah Has Regarded (Hashabiah) and the Ascent to the Armory, we find the brethren of Fortress (Keilah) working under Bavai, ruler of the other half of Keilah and son of Henadad. Bavai translates to "my goings," and his father's name, Henadad, to "favor of Hadad."[xxii] Bavai could be of Persian origin.

Jah has regarded our comings and our goings. He watches over us for our good. What comfort do you find in the following verses?

Psalm 121:1–2

Psalm 121:8

2 Chronicles 16:9

How does God watch over us? Tell of a time you know He was watching over you.

DAY FIVE

EZER: ASCENT TO THE ARMORY AT THE BUTTRESS

NEHEMIAH 3:19

Working just beyond My Goings (Bavai), we locate Ezer son of Jeshua, the leader in Mizpah, working on the Ascent to the Armory and buttress. Ezer's name means "treasure."[xxiii] He is the son of Jeshua (He Will Save)[xxiv] and ruler of Mizpah (Watchtower). Jeshua is a name for Jesus. He is our strong tower; He did save—Jesus is our Savior. We are His treasure, and He is ours (2 Corinthians 4:7).

The Ascent to the Armory at the buttress was where there would have been an angle in the wall. Buttress means "corner or turning" of the wall. It would have been a defensible position, as well as arms storage.[xxv] It is another prophetic picture for us. As we ascend in faith and trust in Jesus, we become clothed in protective armor (Ephesians 6:10–17). We also become equipped with weapons for warfare (2 Corinthians 10:3–4). As we grow in Christ, we learn how to possess our call and authority in Him (Ephesians 1:3–2:7). As we behold Him as our Treasure and know we are His, we stand secure.

How does Jesus relate to Ezer and Jeshua?

Discuss how the ascent of the armory is a prophetic picture for Christians today. How do you see this in the Church and your own life?

NEHEMIAH 3:20

Beyond Treasure (Ezer), we encounter Baruch (Blessed), earnestly repairing the next section.[xxvi] He is the son of Zabbai (Pure).[xxvii] He puts integrity into his work between the buttress and the house of Eliashib. Why is he Blessed (Baruch)? He is born of Purity (Zabbai) and works toward the door of the house of God Will Restore (Eliashib), the high priest.

You see the progression. When we receive Jeshua, Jesus our Salvation, we are born anew in the Spirit, into purity, and this purity makes us blessed. When we live in our blessing, we put integrity and excellence into everything we do for the Lord Jesus, our Restorer and High Priest (Hebrews 7:22–28).

Write the progression seen in these verses. How do they relate to your life?

How do you respond to seeing these truths embedded in building the wall?

MEREMOTH: HOUSE OF ELIASHIB
NEHEMIAH 3:21

Meremoth is our next builder. We have seen his name before. The last time we saw him, he built just beyond the Fish Gate. Now he is building the high priest's home. We will not spend much time on him since we have already covered this. Instead, we will review his, his father's, and his grandfather's names in this order: Heights, Flame Of Jah, and Thorn.

We see Heights (Meremoth), descended from Flame Of Jah (Urijah), moved from the Fish Gate on the northwestern part of the wall to the high priest's home on the eastern side, just south of the center point. He has gone from hanging out with the fishermen to hanging out at the high priest's place.

I cannot help but think of Jesus telling Peter and Andrew that if they followed Him, He would make them fishers of men (Matthew 4:18, 19). We, too, are called to be fishers of men. Once we were lost, but somehow we heard of Jesus from one of His fishers. Once we are hooked on Him and hanging out in His presence, He calls us also to turn and be fishers of men (Matthew 28:18–20).

By the way, let's remember the translation for Eliashib is God Will Restore. Jesus, our High Priest, did not just leave heaven, live a perfect life on earth, and die on the cross to save us from hell. He also rose again, making the way to restore us to our created purpose. The more we live our purpose, the closer and more intimate we become with our High Priest. We are in both places—temporal and spiritual.

We are not only freed from destruction. What else do you learn from the following verses, and how do they apply to this section of Nehemiah's wall?

Ephesians 2:10

1 Peter 2:5

How do you see this in your life today? How are you living out the life of a fisher of men (humankind) as part of the holy priesthood? Is this a new thought for you?

How do you see this coming out as a natural part of your daily life? How would you like to see it in the future?

Who is the most outstanding example of this in your life? Why?

PRIESTS AND MEN OF THE PLAIN

NEHEMIAH 3:22

These priests were descendants of Joined To (Levi) and would have lived in the plain around Jerusalem. They would most likely be the officers of the temple and the singers who lived nearby for ease of access to the temple. Here we see they did not assume that their positions elevated them above the hard work of repairing the wall of their beloved city. We also see their humility in simply working on a nondescript wall area. They just lent their hands to the work right in front of them.

What example do these Levites set for you?

How does this continue the thought that those in Christ are priests of the Lord? How can we apply this to church today? How do you apply it to your own life?

Nehemiah and the East Wall

Week Six / Day One

Nehemiah 3:23–32

Following the priests are Benjamin (Son of the Right Hand) and Hashub (Intelligent), working right where they live.[i] It is all we know of these men. Sometimes our given name and occupation will be what we are known for; this is good if our purpose is to the glory of God (Proverbs 27:2).

What should we work for, according to Matthew 5:16?

We might get a mention, but what belongs to Jesus, according to 2 Peter 3:18?

May I say it is intelligent to be at God's right hand? What docs Isaiah 41:10 say about God's right hand? Where else would you want to be?

Where did these men work? How can you apply this to your life/service in the kingdom?

For what are they known? How can you apply that to your life?

AZARIAH: BY HIS HOUSE
NEHEMIAH 3:23

Beyond Son of the Right Hand (Benjamin) and Intelligent (Hashub) worked Azariah son of Maaseiah, son of Ananiah. He also built by his own house along the wall. Here we have Jah Has Helped (Azariah), son of Work Of Jah (Maaseiah), son of Jah Has Covered (Ananiah)—three generations displaying faith and reliance upon God's faithfulness, goodness, and mercy.[ii]

Jah Has Helped (Azariah) is another obscure name building along an obscure wall section. Nevertheless, his contribution helped to complete the whole. Never discount your little activities for the Lord when no one sees or acknowledges them. God sees. I wonder if this was why they could do such work for Him, knowing His help, work, and covering.

Look up Matthew 6:3, 4. What do you learn about the right hand in this verse? How does that contrast to the right hand we looked at earlier?

What does it say about deeds done when and where no one else sees them?

On what did these men rely? How does that look in your life?

What is good about being an obscure human working in an obscure area for God?

Not only does God see your obedience to Him, He sees the bigger picture. You might only see a few bricks, but He sees the whole wall!

Read 1 Peter 5:6 and note the directive. What is the promise, and how does this apply to our discussion? How have you seen this work in your life?

BINNUI: HOUSE OF AZARIAH TO THE TURNING OF THE WALL
NEHEMIAH 3:24

Here, we meet Binnui son of Henadad building this last section of obscure wall from the house of Azariah (Jah Has Helped) to the buttress. More specifically, by translation, we have Built Up (Binnui), son of Favor of Hadad (Henadad), repairing the wall up to the buttress where the king's court begins.[iii]

Binnui's father carried his father's favor, and he was named Built Up. Imagine if we carried ourselves as though we had our Father's favor and used it to build up our children. They, too, would be known as built up. Too often we carry dysfunction from our childhood or past poor decisions into our future relationships. Whether with friendships, marriage, or our children, we can unintentionally perpetuate cycles we could stop with us.

We can walk in generational curses or blessings. However our lives begin, it is our choice how they will continue and end. Did you know you have the authority to break generational curses when you are in Christ (Ephesians 1:20–2:6)? It does not matter how they came. You do not have to follow your earthly family's path. You can stand up and claim your rightful inheritance in Christ. Knowing who you are in Christ gives you authority to command the chains/bondage of generational sins and curses to leave you and your family line. Invite the Holy Spirit to come in and fill those places with the truth of who you truly are in Christ, then rejoice in the favor of God on your life. Then you will be built up, knowing the favor of your heavenly Father more fully, more abundantly.

What is the result of carrying the favor of your heavenly Father? How do we extend this to our children?

What is a generational curse, and how can one be broken?

Prayerfully seek Jesus to show you any stronghold(s) in your life from which He is ready to help you break free. If you are meeting with a group, share what came to mind. Pray for each other and break the curses off of your lives in Jesus's name. Write a testimony below of your experience or questions. God is good; He will help you.

Day Two

PALAL: TOWER OF THE KING'S UPPER HOUSE
NEHEMIAH 3:25

Palal, the son of Uzai, had the honor of building this next section. His name means "judge," and his father's name means "strong"—a couple of forceful names appropriate for where he built.[iv] We see a son born of one named Strong (Uzai) being named Judge (Palal). The question arises: what kind of judge? One who is fair and impartial, or one who was hard-nosed or, worse yet, available for a price?

We encounter Judge (Palal) building at the tower of the king's upper house. Scholars believe it to be David's palace.[v] The king was the judge in David's time. It is a beautiful reminder of our King, who is also our Judge. Let us look at our next builder before we finish this thought.

PEDAIAH: THE PRISON COURT
NEHEMIAH 3:25

Beyond Judge (Palal), we discover Pedaiah son of Parosh, working most likely on the wall at the prison court. Pedaiah means "Jah has ransomed."[vi] His father's name means "flea."[vii] What a strange transition. Maybe Flea's father chose his name because of how he felt under the Babylonian and then Persian empires. Remember how the spies who checked out the Promised Land for Moses returned and said, "We were like grasshoppers in our own sight" (Numbers 13:33)? How much more may this man have felt like a flea amongst such a great nation.

These are just the kind of odds in which God shows Himself able. Here is a man named Flea (Parosh) naming his son Jah Has Ransomed (Pedaiah). He has seen the hope God has given. His situation seems to have transitioned from impossible odds to God's ability. What joy. Jah Has Ransomed!

We want to tie together the two men working and building side by side at the king's place and the prison court. What an interesting scene. In this location, we have side by side those in prison and the ruler of the land, who holds power over life and death, bondage and freedom. The two men working in this area are Judge (Palal) and Jah Has Ransomed (Pedaiah). Do you see where I am going here?

Read John 3:18. What condition are we in without Jesus?

What happens when we come before the Judge?
Romans 3:23

1 Timothy 2:6

John 3:16

2 Timothy 4:8

We, without Jesus, are in the prison court. We are no more than fleas. Already condemned, our lives are without value (John 3:18). We come before the Judge and are found guilty without Christ. Nevertheless, God, our righteous Judge, gave His Son to pay our penalty, though we stand guilty (2 Timothy 4:8; Romans 3:23; 1 Timothy 2:6). Jah has ransomed you and me through the precious blood of Jesus (John 3:16). He has opened the prison doors and set us free. Our strong Judge has transformed us from "flea" to "ransomed." We are made new in Christ Jesus (2 Corinthians 5:17). Can I hear a shout of praise? Better yet, write a paragraph of praise to the One who set you free.

Tell of a time you experienced "impossible odds" turning into "God is able."

NETHINIM: WATER GATE TOWARD THE EAST
NEHEMIAH 3:26

Following Jah Has Ransomed (Pedaiah) were the Nethinim of Ophel. The Nethinim were temple servants, formerly known as Gibeonites. The Gibeonites had dressed like they were from a faraway land and tricked Israel and Joshua into making a treaty with them. Joshua and his men thought there would be no harm since the Gibeonites were from so far away. They did not seek God for direction and made a treaty with the people of the land, which God had commanded Israel not to do. Joshua subjected them to servitude, making them woodcutters and water carriers in Israel (Joshua 9:1–27).

When Jesus has ransomed us, while we become His co-heirs, we also become willingly enslaved to Him (Romans 6:16–18). The term "bondservant" is found eight times in the New Testament. Paul, James, Peter, and Jude call themselves bondservants of Christ; so do I (Romans 1:1; Galatians 1:10; Philippians 2:7; Colossians 4:12; Titus 1:1; James 1:1; 2 Peter 1:1; Jude 1:1). I hope you do, as well.

The Gibeonites later became known as Nethinim, meaning "one given."[viii] They had been slaves of Joined To (the Levites). They lived at Ophel, which means "hill," with a root meaning of "fortress."[ix] These slaves who had come into subjection as Israel began to take the Promised Land were still with them. They repaired as far as the Water Gate and the projecting tower.

The Water Gate was on the eastern wall. It was the entrance through which water was carried for temple use. One commentator suggests this eastern gate was "for the escape of the superfluous water from temple reservoirs, or for the introduction of water from the Kidron Valley when the reservoirs were low."[x] Ezekiel had a vision of a river of water coming from the temple to the east (Ezekiel 47:1–12).

What does Ezekiel describe in verse 12?

Read John 7:37–39. This is a repeat, but let us take it in the context of this portion of scripture. List the main points.

Jesus said, "If anyone thirsts, let him come to Me and drink. He who believes in Me, as the Scripture has said, out of his heart will flow rivers of living water. 'But this He spoke concerning the Spirit, whom those believing in Him would receive; for the Holy Spirit was not yet given, because Jesus was not yet glorified" (John 7:37–39). Jesus received His glory.

Are you experiencing rivers of living water today? Ask Jesus in what measure you are in the river. Are you ankle-deep, knee-deep, waist-deep, or are you all in—over your head? Ask Him what level He wants you at, and invite Him to take you there. Come on—a flowing river of life! Take a deep dive; you will never be the same. You will never regret it.

Finally, these Given Ones (Nethinim), the temple servants, repaired the great tower. It would be an elevated stage or pulpit. It is possibly the position from which Ezra addressed the people (Ezra 10:9). It is a beautiful picture, these Given servants of the temple providing the stage from which their captors would speak. As His servants, we should also provide the platform from which He can address the crowds. How? By living our lives intentionally. We need to connect every aspect of our lives with purpose and expectation. The next time you run errands, expect Jesus to show up, then watch for the platform to appear.

What do you learn about the Nethinim in these verses?

What does it mean to be a bondservant, and how does it relate to Jesus?

What is the river of living water Jesus spoke of, according to John? Are you carrying rivers of living water in you today?

TEKOITES: FROM THE GREAT PROJECTING TOWER AS FAR AS THE WALL OF OPHEL
NEHEMIAH 3:27

Here, following Jah Has Ransomed (Pedaiah) and the Given Ones (Nethinim), we again find Trumpet Blast (the Tekoites) repairing the wall of Ophel. They had previously repaired the northwestern section of the wall (Nehemiah 3:5). Their nobles were not helpful there, and here we see no mention of them. Instead, we see Trumpet Blast (the Tekoites) not letting their leaders slow them down. Hopefully, they were not doing double duty to compensate for their leaders'shortcomings. Hopefully, they served out of zeal for their city, "whose builder and maker is God" (Hebrews 11:9, 10).

I have one more note about Trumpet Blast (the Tekoites). The placement of their work on the wall around this city is exciting. We first saw them building near the beginning of our study, and we see them here again toward the end of the project. God announces what He will do when He is about to do it (Amos 3:7). Moses used trumpets to assemble and direct the congregation of Israel (Numbers 10:2). A long trumpet blast sounded before God spoke the Ten Commandments audibly to the children of Israel (Exodus 19:16). So it must be significant for Trumpet Blast (the Tekoites) to herald both the start and finish, just as it will be when Jesus returns for His bride (1 Thessalonians 4:16).

How should shortcomings in leadership affect your work?

What do you find interesting or significant about the Tekoites' (Trumpet Blast's) placement on the wall?

When will the trumpet blast for the final time on the earth?

DAY THREE

PRIESTS: THE HORSE GATE

NEHEMIAH 3:28

After Trumpet Blast (the Tekoites), the priests made repairs in front of their houses at and past the Horse Gate. As mentioned before, priests are descendants of Levi, or Joined To. The primitive root of *priests* is "to mediate."[xi] God's mediators (priests) worked and repaired where they lived. Isn't this what mediators do? They work to repair broken associations. They represent both sides impartially, intending to restore them to relationship.

Mediate (priests) worked near Trumpet Blast (the Tekoites). God was calling Israel and the lost to Himself at the Horse Gate, where travelers of all nations entered, and horses came for refreshing.[xii] All who come at the trumpet blast of God find a Mediator in Jesus, our High Priest (1 Timothy 2:5; Hebrews 8:6; 9:15; 12:24). He stands at the door and knocks; He seeks to be invited in (Revelation 3:20). Once we invite Him in through faith, we too find times of refreshing (Acts 3:19).

What do mediators do; what is their goal? How do we relate this to us today?

Who entered through the Horse Gate? What did they find there? How does this apply to evangelism and the lost coming to Jesus? How is this reflected in your life?

ZADOK: OVER AGAINST HIS HOUSE
NEHEMIAH 3:29

Making repairs beyond the Horse Gate at the position of his own house along the city wall is Zadok son of Immer. Zadok means "just," and Immer means "talkative."[xiii]

What does Ecclesiastes 5:3 tell us about talkative?

What are we warned about in Proverbs 10:19?

The word *just* is interesting in its uses. Sometimes you might feel you are just not enough or you just made it. However, in Zadok's case, *just* means "to be morally right, cleansed, or righteous."[xiv] Sometimes you might feel unworthy to claim this name, Just.

What do these scriptures reveal about your right to claim the name Just?
Romans 3:24

Romans 5:1

It is not for us to achieve; it is who and how we become when we believe in Jesus in faith—faith believes. You are just and righteous—cleansed before Him. Do you believe this today? It is true if you have received Jesus as your Savior.

According to Romans 5:1, we are justified by faith. What more do you learn about justification from the following verses?
Romans 6:4

Romans 6:6

Galatians 5:16

Colossians 2:6

It is *just* for you to walk in this newness of life. What does justification mean? Can we earn it? How are we justified?

How is Just (Zadok) a natural progression from the discussion in the previous section about inviting Jesus in and experiencing refreshing?

SHEMAIAH: THE EAST GATE
NEHEMIAH 3:29

Beyond Judge (Zadok) repaired Shemaiah son of Shechaniah, keeper of the East Gate. Jah Has Heard (Shemaiah) is his name; he is the man repairing the East Gate.[xv] His father's name means Jah Has Dwelt or Dweller with Jah (Shechaniah).[xvi] The one who dwells with God, God hears. For God to dwell with one is for one to be blessed (Genesis 9:27; Exodus 29:45; Revelation 3:20, 21:3).

Jah Has Heard (Shemaiah), keeper of the East Gate, worked to repair the gate. He had been a keeper of a broken gate. Now, with the arrival of Jah Comforts (Nehemiah), he has found permission and courage to do the work to repair this gate he has been keeping. It is time for the Church to stop keeping broken gates; it is time to rise to repair. Jah has heard, and He has sent Nehemiahs amongst us. The question is, will we rise and repair amid opposition, or will we continue in comfort and feigned peace as we keep watch over broken gates? What about the gates of broken dreams and failed attempts? Will we allow them to relegate us to watchers? Or will we let them catalyze us to rise to new heights, new challenges, and new victories?

What can you glean from the names of Shemaiah and his father?

What did Jah Has Heard (Shemaiah) receive with the arrival of Jah Comforts (Nehemiah)? Why was this important?

What is true of those who watch over broken gates?

How have you let broken dreams and failed attempts affect you—for good or for bad? How do you turn them into catalysts for the more and the better?

How can you apply Romans 8:29–30 to these experiences?

What comfort do you take from Hebrews 12:1–2?

DAY FOUR

After Jah Has Heard (Shemaiah), Hananiah son of Shelemiah and Hanun, sixth son of Zalaph, repaired along the wall. Hananiah means "Jah has favored."[xvii] His father is Shelemiah, which means "thank offering of Jah."[xviii] Hanun means "favored."[xix] His father's name, Zalaph, means "wound."[xx] So we have Jah Has Favored (Hananiah) working alongside another whose name also ascribes favor to him.

Interestingly, the second favored man came from a man whose name meant "wound." We can surmise that one came from hardship, while the other came with faith and favor. Children are a heritage from the Lord (Psalm 127:3). Maybe Wound (Zalaph) had begun to understand God's heart toward him when he named his sixth son Favored (Hanun).

In some seasons we can only see the chaos of our past—maybe even our present. Then another season comes, and we see God enter the picture—for the first time or to call us to new levels of maturity, as He invites us to refocus our gaze. Whether this represents forgiveness or acceptance of what has been, a time comes to let it go under the blood of Jesus. It is a time to turn our gaze heavenward and "set [our minds] on things above, not on things on the earth" (Colossians 3:1–3).

Before I came to Christ, I went through a short-lived abusive marriage. I was in my very young twenties, and when it was over, an internal voice told me I was supposed to live as a bitter divorcée. It was also a time when it was trendy to go to counseling, so I went, because it was modern. The counselor I saw recommended a book for me to read. Unfortunately, it was full of profanity, so I did not finish reading it. Even as a non-Christian, I found it offensive. However, I was desperate for an answer, and I found it early in the book.

The miraculous piece of information this book gave me was that it was within my power to choose my response to my complicated life circumstances. I felt I had to walk the road laid out before me, but this author assured me I could choose any path I wanted; I was in control. I instantly chose a new approach, and my life was immeasurably better. I learned I could choose to let go. My past did not have to be my identity, and your junk and yuck do not have to be yours. You get to choose.

It seems Satan has no end of broad roads. He tries to get us to set our feet to bitterness, unforgiveness, envy, distress, despair, and more. Jesus, though, gave us a better option. He said, "Enter by the narrow gate" (Matthew 7:13). We now know Jesus is the narrow gate. When we receive salvation, we are on a new path. He gives us new options and the power to use them: purity, forgiveness, generosity, peace, joy, and all of the characteristics of Christ.

What promises do you find in the following scriptures?
Isaiah 61:3

Jeremiah 31:13

Ask Jesus where He wants to turn ashes into beauty, mourning into joy for you today (Isaiah 61:3; Jeremiah 31:13). Are you willing to let the past go and trade for a better future? If not, why not? Spend some time considering this. Sometimes, our negative feelings become our familiar friends, and we fear we will not be able to live without them. Consider who would want you to believe such a lie. Then ask Holy Spirit to help you break free into your new life, to trade your wound for the favor of Jah.

What truth do you glean from the meanings of Hanun's and his father's names?

Regardless of where people come from, what is the hope for every person in Christ? (See the two builders' names for help.)

What must we do with the chaos of our past—maybe even our present lives? How can we do this?

Why do we have the power to choose? How have you chosen to utilize this power in your life?

Is there anything you let go of while reading this section? Write it down and plan to share it, whether meeting in a group or asking God to show you who needs to hear it.

MESHULLAM: IN FRONT OF HIS DWELLING

NEHEMIAH 3:30

Just past Jah Has Favored (Hananiah) and Favored (Hanun) worked Meshullam son of Berechiah. We already discussed these men and their names in verse 4. Meshullam means "allied/friend," and his father's name means "blessing of Jah." The new information we discover here is that he was building in front of his home.

Jah has heard, Jah has favored, and Jesus is our Friend. All these glorious attributes of God's nature dwell with you.

What truths do these scriptures reveal?

1 John 5:14

Psalms 5:12; 30:5

John 15:13–15

These are the attributes of a functional family. We are listened to, favored, and allied in a functional family.

What dwells with you right now, right where you live?

Do you struggle to receive any of the truths in this section? If yes, why do you think they are difficult to receive?

DAY FIVE

Malchijah, a goldsmith or son of a goldsmith, repaired up to the house of the Nethinim and merchants in front of the Miphkad Gate. This text is somewhat confusing, as some translate Malchijah as the son of a goldsmith, and others translate him as the goldsmith. Either way works, as fathers handed professions down to sons; it can be true both ways. Malchijah means "king of Jah" or "my king is Jah."[xxi] Another word for goldsmith is "refiner."[xxii]

Another My King Is Jah (Malchijah) made repairs at the Tower of the Furnaces. However, we do not know if this was the same person because we do not have genealogy to compare. This man named My King Is Jah (Malchijah) was a Refiner (goldsmith), most likely the son of a refiner.

Malachi 3:2–4 speaks of God as a refining fire. What does Malachi say He will do, and what will be the result? In Christ, we are a royal priesthood. How does this apply to us?

What do James and Peter say about spiritual refining?
James 1:2–4

1 Peter 1:6–7

Peter lists the characteristics of a purified life in Christ in his second book (2 Peter 1:5–7). It begins with faith, just as we started with belief when we entered the Sheep Gate at the beginning of this chapter. List the other virtues.

Peter brings us full circle to the pinnacle of our Christian existence: brotherly love. "Since you have purified your souls in obeying the truth through the Spirit in sincere love of the brethren, love one another fervently with a pure heart" (1 Peter 1:22).

We will all continue to go through hard times. What will change is our having a Friend to lean on as we walk through them. How are you meeting your trials today? Are you hoping they pass you by, living in fear and hiding? Are you fighting in the natural realm? Or are you surrendering it all to Jesus? Are you trusting Him to see you through as you rely on His promises and draw near to Him?

I am not discounting the difficulty of the trials you go through. I have had my share of seemingly insurmountable trials. However, I know I always come out better than before the trial began, and I have grown in ways I would not have otherwise. I do not have to be grateful for the trials, but I do get to be grateful to the great God who sees me through them and somehow makes me better and stronger for them. One truth I can rely on when trials come is that though He does not always save me from the trial, He never makes me walk through it alone.

My King Is Jah (Malchijah) and the Refiner (goldsmith) built at the Miphkad Gate. This gate is mentioned nowhere else in Scripture. The Nethinim (temple servants) and the merchants most likely stayed there. Miphkad means "appointed place."[xxiii] It may be the appointed place where merchants were to enter and exit, possibly to be counted. The root of "census" also lies within the word. It would be a place where they accounted for everyone who entered.

What does the word goldsmith mean? How can you relate this to Jesus and Scripture? How have you seen this in your life?

As what does Malachi speak of God? What would He do, and what would be the result?

What does Peter tell us life's trials are? What is the result for those in Christ?

What is the pinnacle of our Christian experience, according to Peter?

How are you meeting your trials today?

THE GOLDSMITHS AND MERCHANTS: BETWEEN THE UPPER ROOM AND THE SHEEP GATE
NEHEMIAH 3:32

Our final stretch of the wall between the upper room at the corner and the Sheep Gate is where the goldsmiths and merchants made repairs. They were the artistic ones who brought beauty and sweet aromas to the city of God. The goldsmiths were not merely refiners of precious metals; they were craftsmen who would make beautiful jewelry and other items to admire and enjoy.

Jesus is our refiner and purifier. "And according to the law almost all things are purified with blood, and without shedding of blood, there is no remission" (Hebrews 9:22). "Christ was offered once to bear the sins of many. To those who eagerly wait for Him, He will appear a second time, apart from sin, for salvation" (Hebrews 9:28). We are made pure by His blood. Our value is restored before the Father.

The merchants would bring perfumes and spices to sell in the city. Imagine the aromas they carried with them. We, too, carry an aroma when we are in Christ. To one, "we are the aroma of death leading to death, and to the other, the aroma of life leading to life" (2 Corinthians 2:16). When we are washed by the blood and come into a real and personal relationship with Jesus, it changes us. It begins at the Sheep Gate and finishes with the fragrant aroma of a sweet-smelling sacrifice, a life fully surrendered to God (Romans 12:1).

In what way is Jesus our refiner and purifier?

What do we who are in Christ carry?

How does coming into a real and personal relationship with Jesus change us? How has it changed you?

We have come full circle around the wall. What stood out to you most about your journey around the wall? How will you apply it to your life?

Congratulations on completing the journey around the wall with Nehemiah and me. I am amazed at how God has placed a redemptive story in the names and places around this wall of Jerusalem. Let it sink in—the purposefulness of our God. He is able beyond what we can think or imagine. His fervent love for us explodes on the pages of Scripture for us to see daily. Take some time to sit in awe of Him, then write Him a love letter from your heart. I'll meet you again next week for chapter seven and a closer look at enemy tactics.

Nehemiah and Enemy Tactics

Nehemiah 4:1–23

Chapter three gave us a wonderful prophetic glimpse of salvation and transformation. Chapter four continues our journey as we see Israel's enemies awakened to what was happening in Jerusalem. This chapter allows us to see spiritual growth in action as Nehemiah and the Israelites continue to work amid their enemies 'attempts to disrupt them. We will see and understand our enemy's tactics and how to respond to them. We will also look at how the enemy of our soul responds when he *hears* of advancements in God's kingdom and the strategies he uses to stop kingdom—and personal—growth.

Read James 1:2–4. What does James tell us to do when we fall into various trials? Why? What will be the result?

We met Sanballat and Tobiah in chapter two. They "were deeply disturbed that a man had come to seek the well-being of the children of Israel" (Nehemiah 2:10). Chapter four begins with Sanballat reacting to news that Nehemiah's plan was finding traction and progressing. According to the New King James Version of the Bible, his reaction was fury and indignance.

Scripture reveals another time when someone became indignant. Read Matthew 21:7–15 and note who was indignant and why. (Other translations may say irritated, displeased, incensed, or furious.)

Why do you think this was their reaction?

Do you see this happening in churches today? In what way?

Have you experienced this on either side? What might be the root of such a reaction, and how can we respond to it on whichever side we find ourselves?

It was the crescendo moment in history when Jesus would go to the cross. This pivotal moment would bring salvation to the world and release the Holy Spirit's dispensation and the Church's birth. God was building His kingdom one living stone at a time, and these priests were indignant. They could not recognize Jesus as their Messiah even though He taught with authority and healed all kinds of sickness and disease (Mark 4:23). He had been preaching that the kingdom of God was at hand. These spiritual leaders were too caught up in their culture, traditions, and expectations to see Him.

Nehemiah built with earthly stones, but now all believers make up the building of God as living stones, "a dwelling place for God" (Ephesians 2:21, 22). Here, we see two reactions to building the kingdom. First, we observe the enemy respond with anger and hatred, as he does not want God to win, though He already has. Second, we see the reaction of the comfortable, complacent, religious. Those who have refined their walk with God down to a formula of activity are never pleased when God shows up in power with purpose.

We will see the enemy's tactics as we look at Sanballat, Tobiah, and their friends. We will also see Nehemiah's examples of how to respond to these schemes. However, we will also see, on some level, reactions and activities we might recognize in ourselves.

We are sinners saved by grace, and we are at war with our flesh as we are sanctified day by day (Hebrews 10:14).

Read this text with a heart softened to the Holy Spirit's touch. Allow Him to teach you how to respond to and overcome the enemy as well as the flesh. Be willing to be convicted so you can be set free to soar on new heights with Him. It can only be good to be convicted if we meet it with repentance and surrender. "Therefore, if anyone is in Christ, he is a new creation; old things have passed away; behold, all things have become new" (2 Corinthians 5:17).

How is the enemy's response compared and contrasted with the religious person's response? Did you sense any conviction or confirmation? If yes, how did you respond to it?

Why is it important to be willing to allow Holy Spirit to convict you?

Spend time rejoicing in His goodness. If you are in a trial, thank Him for the spiritual growth He will bring out of it. Trust me; I know this can be challenging at first. If this is too much for you, begin to thank Him for walking through it with you and ask Him to reveal Himself to you in the midst of it. Ask Him to help you stay your eyes on Him, knowing there will be an end to this trial.

DAY TWO

NEHEMIAH 4:1–6

Sanballat's fury and indignation led him to act. He began with words. He mocked, and because he had an audience, we can also say he gossiped. His words were belittling and his actions invited others to join in his destructive behavior. Sanballat said Nehemiah and his people were feeble; he joked they could not fortify themselves or worship there.

The sentence I was most struck by recently was, "Will they revive the stones from the heaps of rubbish?" (Nehemiah 4:2). Revive the stones! We are living stones, and God is reviving us even now. When we are in a crisis, we often think the same way. Can God revive this situation? Can he restore me? The answer is a resounding YES! We see this as Nehemiah builds the wall. We know how it ends; the wall gets built.

What is the good news Jesus shares with us in John 16:33?

What does this mean for you and me? Jesus *will* revive these stones. If we continue to press into Him and rely on Him, He will restore us to our destiny. Jesus is for us and never against us (Romans 8:31). We are His very own special people whom He loves (Titus 2:14). Jesus will not let us down. He will rebuild. He will revive these stones!

How do the truths in the following verses confirm this truth? How do they encourage you today?

Romans 8:31

Titus 2:14

In verse 3, we see how Sanballat's gossip affected his friend. Tobiah, the Ammonite and fellow enemy of Israel, chimed in with disparaging remarks and showed his contempt with words. One man's indignation poured out verbally, inciting his friend to respond in kind (1 Corinthians 15:33). It is indeed this easy. We have a pair of friends commiserating together about their common enemy.

Read 1 Corinthians 15:33 and note how it applies here. How have you seen this apply in your life?

Have you ever sat with a friend over a steaming cup of deliciousness, commiserating over the actions of another friend? We like to call this a safe place to vent. However, safe places to vent do not exist. We have places and times to confess our sins to one another, but I have yet to find scriptures inviting me to pour out my indignation over one person to another (James 5:16).

The key is to take these thoughts captive to the obedience of Christ (1 Corinthians 10:5). Measure them against His Word and His character. Measure your motives. Surrender it all to Christ. What are we to do when we are stuck and cannot make it through on our own? We do not meet with a friend who will agree with all we say and support us unconditionally. What we need at a time like this is someone who is mature in Christ and will tell the truth, even if it hurts a little at first. They will be motivated by an earnest desire for our spiritual growth and reconciliation. They will be a safe place to help us find how to bring our thoughts and emotions to the obedience of Christ and preserve relationships.

This is an opportune time to ask yourself in the presence of the Lord where you let fury and indignation lead you. Is there a situation you need to take care of right now? Are you harboring bitterness, hatred, envy, or other negative emotions toward another individual or group? How will you respond to it today? Ask God to show you where the offense happened, forgive—ask Him to help you—repent of your sin, and ask God to fill you with His Spirit, full to overflowing. Be free from this bondage of sin, which exists only to stifle you spiritually.

What comfort do you find in the comments on living stones?

What will a mature Christian do when you need to talk it out? Do you have someone like this in your life? Are you this person for someone else?

What do you find helpful or not helpful in keeping one another accountable?

Like Sanballat and Tobiah, Satan and his enemy hordes despise the forward motion of the kingdom at every level. They do not see a pile of burned and broken-down stones; they see a potential threat, which enrages them. Nehemiah and the Israelites are examples of how to respond to the enemy's rage. Notice the word "respond."

We see Sanballat and Tobiah *react* to the information they *heard*. We, like Nehemiah, must take a breath and *respond*. It is part of taking every thought captive; it keeps us from reacting out of emotion or flesh. Instead, we are able to respond with the heart of Jesus and the authority Jesus gives us.

Nehemiah's first response is our example of what is always the best first response—he prayed. He went first and directly to God with his troubles and concerns. He also did not pray merely for himself or his ministry calling. He prayed on behalf of all of the people: "Hear, O our God" (Nehemiah 4:4). It is a beautiful example for those called to lead others in the body of Christ. Satan's attacks may come, but leaders never need to set their cares apart from those of the people they lead. The enemy is coming after the whole camp, not just your ministry (1 Corinthians 12:25–17).

Nehemiah's prayer on behalf of the people began with an honest assessment of their situation. He said, "We are despised" (Nehemiah 4:4). It is a short phrase but profound and powerful. His acknowledgment of the truth of the situation shows his humility. It positions him to pray a humble and heartfelt prayer to God the Father, the only one who is able to make the difference in their situation.

Nehemiah continued with a request known as an imprecatory prayer, a basic "go get 'em, God" kind of prayer. Nehemiah asked God to turn the enemies 'plans back on themselves. These are those who rejoiced in Judah's captivity. They were in one of two camps. Either they were locals glad to see them go to exile, or they were transferred to Judah from other lands, as was common under the conquering realms of the time. Either way, these enemies did not want to see God's people restored. Nehemiah asked for them to reap what they had sown: let them reap captivity for mocking and rejoicing in Israel's plight.

Nehemiah then, with sober judgment, confessed his understanding of the situation. Their sin was against God, not against Nehemiah or the people building the wall. Their grievance was with God Most High, who tore down their strongholds and made foolish their idols. He is the one who convicts of sin and calls for repentance. Their animosity raged against Him, whether they understood it or not. Nehemiah did understand, and he released it to God.

How important it is for us to grasp this concept today. Nehemiah understood the work he was there to accomplish was for God, and he understood the deep, dark place from which the attack came. He also understood to whom it was pointed and left it in His capable hands.

What do the following verses teach us about God and our enemy?

Exodus 14:14

2 Corinthians 6:14

1 John 4:4

John 10:10

1 Samuel 17:47

Romans 12:9

The workers' other response to the enemy's seething hatred and rumbling grumblings is another example for us to follow. They continued to do the work they found in front of them. At this point, the enemy's fury was just a lot of hot air. There was nothing to do but ignore their enemies and continue what the Lord had given them to do. They could have put down their tools and stopped the work to debate and argue—even to try to lead them to faith. But the workers did not. They did not allow the opposition to distract them.

We only have to go to social media for a moment to see this work the opposite way. I used to read threads of debate out of curiosity until I became sick to my stomach over the cruel words people exchange with each other. Neither one is any longer trying to debate. They are only trying to be heard and win the conversation. Meanwhile, others chime in, and you can tell they are defending their friend more than they are the topic, which grows from there. No one accomplishes anything except maybe shortening their list of friends.

Nehemiah and the people did not let their enemies' tactics distract them from the work. They did not react in the heat of the moment. Instead, they spent their energies on the task at hand, and their reward was that the wall rose up to about half of its height all the way around (Nehemiah 4:6).

We will reap what we sow (Galatians 6:7–8). If we sow into the chaos, we will reap chaos. If we sow into the kingdom, we will reap kingdom rewards. Our good boundaries will keep our enemy at bay and our hearts close to God's own.

What a beautiful example to follow, both for leader and laity. When enemies rumble, pray. When the atmosphere carries threatening words, do not let it distract you from what you do for the Lord. Do not give the enemy the satisfaction of pulling you off task to join in pointless arguments or debates. You have no one to convince; just be confident and set yourself to the task before you. Leave the rest in God's hands. It is His battle to fight. It is our wall to build.

Focus on building His kingdom, and He will take care of the rest. See how He will miraculously provide as you stay focused on the last directive He called you to. Do not let the enemy bring chaos or confusion. If you notice these, know from where they come and follow Nehemiah's example: acknowledge it with honesty, pray, leave it in God's hands, and have a mind to do what you were doing before it showed up. Also, look up and acknowledge God's divine blessing in your work to glorify Him.

What did Nehemiah and the Israelites do in the face of enemy tactics? How does this speak to your life?

Why is taking a breath and responding to a situation so important?

What is always the best first response? Why? Give an example from your own life.

What is imprecatory prayer? Is it okay to pray these prayers today? Why or why not?

Against whom did Sanballat and Tobiah sin? How did this revelation help Nehemiah know how to pray? Why is this an important concept to understand as a Christ follower?

What did Israel do in the face of their enemies' "hot air" rumblings and grumblings? What was the result? How is this an example for you?

Note the enemy tactics and Nehemiah's response(s) in this section. Be specific.

DAY THREE

NEHEMIAH 4:7–9

Nehemiah's enemies far underestimated the people of God because they did not understand the Divine. Their own words betrayed their disbelief in the Israelites' ability to rebuild the wall. They saw Judah and Israel as defeated foes scattered among the nations. They had no worries about their ability to restore a wall, let alone a nation and a people, so they mocked and gossiped.

To their surprise, they heard Nehemiah's wall was progressing. Suddenly, they had to come to terms with the tenacity of their enemy, the Jews, to accomplish this. Their hatred and, might I suggest, fear delivered them to the next level. They moved from gossip and slander to plotting psychological and physical warfare.

The plan increased in severity, and the number of opposing forces increased as the Ashdodites added to their number. It was a big deal. These people building the wall were not warriors. They were regular people with regular jobs living regular lives. They were either left over from the exile or returned from exile. Either way, by history, they were a broken people group dispersed throughout a conqueror's land. The fact that they did not panic at the first signs of the enemy's rumblings is much more impressive when we understand the real threat posed by the surrounding nations. However, their next opportunity to trust God in a storm was about to come upon them.

Their enemies began to deploy a new tactic to accompany their seething rage over the advancement of God's kingdom. This time, it was not just Sanballat leading the group; they "*all* . . . conspired together" (Nehemiah 4:8 *italics mine*). Those who once were rivals became bonded by hatred. They devised a plot to intimidate, confuse, and even bring physical violence to the city where God's people were doing the work.

It is still much the same today. Our enemy will come at us with rumors and gossip. He will attempt to turn people against us or stir up our enemies. When we overcome, he loves to try to confuse us. If he can take our eyes off of our purpose for just a moment, he can get a foothold into our thoughts. Just like Peter walking on water and becoming distracted by the what-ifs, the enemy can cause us to lose focus and sink, too—if we let him (Matthew 14:28–31). We have a Savior who has overcome and has promised we, too, will overcome (John 16:33; 1 John 5:4). He will reach out and steady us as soon as we cry out to Him.

This is what Nehemiah did. He heard the report, and he and his group of workers prayed. They cried out to God for protection, and they also took action. They did not merely pray and wait for God to move. They set a plan in place; Nehemiah set a twenty-four-hour watch against them. There would be no sneaking in. The watchmen would boldly announce their enemy's arrival.

Don't you know Satan loves to lurk in the shadow of familiarity? He does not come to us in the open; he comes as an angel of light (2 Corinthians 11:14). This is why we take every thought captive. It is why we have a devotional life and walk in step with God's Spirit. We must live tuned-in to have the spiritual discernment only the Holy Spirit can give us. Our watch is a prayerful, spiritual perceiving of enemy tactics. We must live aware of an enemy constantly lurking, seeking an opportunity. It is not a watch of trepidation but a preparation to overcome an already defeated foe. We go from victory to victory.

Do not let fear grip you at the thought of a prowling enemy. A spirit of fear is not from God (2 Timothy 1:7). Ours is a spirit of triumph. God has already won the war; it is simply ours to know this and live as overcomers. How do we watch? We pray and have an intimate experience with our God. He is alive and accessible all the time—all. He is never sleeping or too busy to be bothered by our needs, prayers, or conversations. The best way to defeat enemy tactics is to live intimately with God. Know what the Word says about you. Know who and how He is to you, for you, and through you. Know your enemy is defeated, without a doubt. Simple. The more we know the genuine, the easier it is to recognize the counterfeit.

Look up the following verses and note how they apply to Nehemiah and you.

1 Peter 5:8

1 Peter 5:9

1 John 4:4

1 John 5:4

1 John 5:5

Nehemiah's enemies did not believe the Israelites could rebuild the wall. Why? How does this help you understand the disbelief you encounter? How will this help you navigate the nay-sayers?

Nehemiah's enemies increased; at this point, who else entered the narrative? Why was this a big deal?

What plot did they conspire to bring about? How is this a progression of hostile activity toward the Israelites?

What is one way the enemy gets a foothold in our minds? What can we do about it?

What examples does Nehemiah set for responding to these new enemy tactics? How can you emulate these today?

It is not a watch of _____, but a _____

to _____ an already _____ foe.

What is the best way to defeat enemy tactics? Share a time when you did this successfully or a time when you did not. Finally, talk about what challenges you experience in overcoming enemy tactics.

DAY FOUR

What do you see as an enemy tactic in verse 10?

How did this affect the work?

How did their view of the work change?

According to verse 11, how did the enemy's tactics go to the next level?

We encounter the next tactic of the enemy disguised in the words of the people of Judah in verses 10 and 11. They were discouraged. They had allowed their enemies 'rumors and threats to take their eyes off the prize. Rather than a mind to work they had minds focused on the workload. Jesus said His burden is easy and light (Matthew 11:30). This is very true when we keep our hearts established in heaven and our eyes on our hope in Him. We *must* know: If He calls us, He equips us (2 Timothy 3:17). Jesus, the author and finisher of our faith, will not call us to anything without a plan to bring it to fulfillment (Hebrews 12:2). Great joy comes with overcoming, and He has come to give us life abundant (Luke 1:45; John 10:10)! Lauren Daigle's song "Look Up Child" fits here.

We see the people of Judah coming to Nehemiah and giving a report in the hearing of other workers stating their case against the call and plan of God. Why? They were discouraged, and their discouragement was rooted in fear because of the rumors of the enemy's plans. These fear-filled Judahites reported that since Nehemiah had set a twenty-four-hour watch against their enemies, Sanballat and crews escalated from "confuse and terrify" to a plot for murder. Those who once had a mind to work began to think the work was an impossible burden because they were so affected by the threat.

145

Yes, this would be a scary experience. However, Proverbs tells us this is the cry of a lazy person. "The lazy man says, 'There is a lion outside! I shall be slain in the streets'" (Proverbs 22:13). The complainers said the work was too hard. We will always find excuses for why the labor is too much. Either it is too hard, too extensive, too much for the workforce, or too threatened by resistance. These were the basic complaints of this group.

Another interesting detail about this group of fearmongers is where they lived. Verse 12 reveals the location of the Jews who came with disparaging reports to hinder the work of God. They lived near their enemies or even amongst them.

The Israelites' location among foreign peoples was based on how the foreign rulers had dispersed the conquered people groups. When a land was conquered, the victors moved the inhabitants to other regions and replaced them with people from other conquered nations. This guarded against uprisings, which is why several people groups are mentioned in Sanballat's horde of enemy conspirators. Technically, we see a mixed people living in Judah. However, we also see they still lived within their individual people groups.

It is a spiritual picture of how believers live today. The warrior-servants building the wall represent those who dwell near God today, experiencing a daily relationship with Him and living in obedience. Those who live on the outskirts near the enemy's camp, mixing with the enemy, are more susceptible to enemy influence. They become conduits of his activity as they become quicker to look at the crisis and not the Creator. They will see the enemy's power, forgetting he is a created being and no match for our matchless God Almighty.

Which of the scriptures mentioned for overcoming discouragement speak loudest to your heart? Why? How is the physical location of the Israelites a spiritual picture of how believers live today?

What life experiences might draw or drive a believer to live in the outer camp? What can draw them back in? What can they do to draw closer to God?

How does this speak to you where you are today? How are you drawing closer and inviting others to do the same?

At this moment, the enemy may have gotten more than was planned. Their plot for murder to stop God's work produced a psychological response which sent Nehemiah's own people to discourage him and the faithful workers. His people came to him with predictions of doom and reasons why this must not be God's plan: it was too hard and dangerous. They repeated their doom and gloom ten times and planted a seed of doubt in some. Remember, the wall stood finished up to half its height when this latest conspiracy came to light.

They had already accomplished half of the job. Clearing away the debris must have made the work much more challenging in the beginning. It was undoubtedly more difficult to imagine the finished product from the start than from the middle. Nevertheless, this was when those who lived on the outskirts, on the edges of relationship with Jerusalem, began gossiping about threats and trying to stop God's work. Why? They let earthly voices override heavenly calling. They forgot for a moment whom they served. They forgot that this and every other battle belongs to the Lord (1 Samuel 17:47). He will finish with or without us. We can be an encouraging part of a great movement or join with enemy voices and discourage those around us.

How do you want to use your voice—your influence? How do you want to be influenced? As the old saying goes, "Garbage in, garbage out." It is true spiritually. Whatever we allow to influence us will soon influence others through us. What have you been letting into your spirit and soul lately? Are you spending ample time in God's Word? Are you experiencing Him in relationship through prayer and listening for His voice?

Did you know He will speak to your spirit if you wait and listen? He wants to have a relationship with you. Won't you plan a time to meet with Him daily and practice presence with Him?

The late pastor Ron Mehl used to say, "If it is not over your head, it is probably not God." Maybe your wall is halfway finished all around. Do not give up now! Rejoice over the obstacles you have already overcome, and let those testimonies carry you to your finish line. Our enemy is a defeated foe. Who cares what he plans and plots? Remember, God knows the beginning from the end, and He has already established a plan to prosper you and not to harm you (Jeremiah 29:11; Isaiah 46:10). Trust in Him. Walk with Him. Dance with Him!

Nehemiah might have rolled his eyes on the inside this time. He had a call from God. Nehemiah had risked his life simply by presenting his thoughts to his king and then again by traveling to Jerusalem to do the work of God. He risked his life in Jerusalem as well, but all along the way, he trusted God to keep him as he obeyed his heart-felt call and duty. The enemy harassed him; this he expected. It is when their own people turn on them that leaders are caught off guard.

People (we) will follow a leader without entirely counting the cost or feeling a need to commit fully. Some today do not even understand the importance of commitment. Some will come to gossip, distracting others from the heavenly and immersing them in the muck and mire of earthly mindsets. But, as in this instance, some are too earthly-minded. They begin to complain about the work, the plan, and the possible adverse outcomes, and they draw the faithful away.

Nehemiah may have struggled at times. He was a cupbearer to the king of Persia, not a master builder or city manager. Nehemiah was a child of God called to do a work greater than himself. He could have thrown the naysayers out, but instead, with a humble heart, he responded to this new situation with a new plan. They would no longer merely keep watch but also position and prepare themselves for battle (Nehemiah 4:13).

What a brilliant strategy, to position people in front of their homes and families. How much harder would they defend their position, knowing they fought not simply for God's people and property but their families and family properties? Also, they would have an intimate communication relationship, making them a more potent fighting force. They would not always need words; a look or body language could express as much as words between them. This kingdom tactic would bond them as a family, a city, and a nation.

Nehemiah then addressed everyone. He left no one out. He addressed the nobles, the leaders, and the people (Nehemiah 4:14). He understood the issue and addressed the problem. Nehemiah realized their whiny complaints came from a spirit of fear birthed in an earthly focus. He understood the need to redirect their attention to God and His ability—to remind them that God would defend them, defeat their enemies, and help them fulfill their calling to build the kingdom for His glory.

What did Nehemiah tell them to remember in verse 14?

What did Moses say to the Israelites in the wilderness before entering the Promised Land? (See Deuteronomy 7:21.)

"Remember the Lord great and awesome" (Nehemiah 4:14). This simple phrase carried national history and testimony. When Moses addressed Israel in the desert before they entered, he spoke to them about life in the Promised Land. He reminded them to consider what the Lord had done for them in Egypt. He said, "You shall not be terrified of them; for the Lord your God, the great and awesome God, is among you" (Deuteronomy 7:21). Nehemiah's words testified to every great work the Lord had ever done for Israel. What better phraseology could Nehemiah have used to remind them of who they were and who their God was for them?

What do you do when you are discouraged and despairing because the enemy has tricked you into gazing upon earthly realities nonexistent in kingdom realities? How long do you commiserate before remembering all the great and wonderful works the Lord has done for you? Is your wall halfway done or halfway from being done? Remember what

God has done and keep your eyes on the goal—in faith in the only God who is able (Deuteronomy 7:21; Revelation 11:7).

What do leaders expect, and what sneaks up on them? How do you respond to these statements?

How did Nehemiah respond to this new situation? What was brilliant about his new strategy? Why?

Where did the Israelites' complaints come from? What did Nehemiah know he needed to do? How did he accomplish it?

Nehemiah did not panic, react, or despair at the news of this new enemy tactic. He responded with wisdom. We see the result in verse 15. All it took for the enemies of God's people to turn away from their evil plot was for God's people to know about it. Did you see it? Just like in verse 1 of this chapter, their actions were based on what they *heard*. While they did not serve the God of Israel, they did seem to respect Him. It is true of our spiritual enemies, as well. They know God; they know Scripture, but they do not submit or surrender to either. They hate everything associated with God. However, when we know our God and Scripture and come to know our enemy's plans, he is already defeated and knows it. One scripture to hold onto is "resist the [enemy], and he will flee" (James 4:7). Stop agreeing with the enemy of your soul and look up!

The other result—the best result—was the people's returning to their work. During the first plot, the people had a mind to work, and they completed the wall up to half its height. Then discouraging voices, threats, and fear disrupted the flow. However, when a strong leader responded wisely, it enabled the people to return to the work of kingdom building. Albeit, they did adjust the workload a bit.

At this point, Nehemiah split the people. Half worked on building the wall, and the other half carried weapons and armor to defend against an attack. Their actions sent a strong and clear message. The enemy would no longer see a weak peasant construction force. Instead, they would see a military presence. They would know the battle was no longer one-sided, and knowing victory was not assured caused them to pause.

Paul tells us in Ephesians to put on the whole armor of God (Ephesians 6:11). When the enemy sees us clothed in the full armor (truth, righteousness, the gospel of peace, faith, salvation, the Word of God, prayer, and the Holy Spirit), he, too, will back down. Our enemy will see we are firm footed and not easily shaken. Yes, he will try at times, but he prefers an easier target. The last verse of this section of Ephesians says, "praying always with all prayer and supplication in the Spirit, being watchful to this end with all perseverance and supplication for the saints" (Ephesians 6:18). This is how we watch today. We armor up, and we pray for other believers, our leaders, and our peers. We persevere in prayer *always*.

We see those who were doing the building also carrying weapons. They built their section of the wall, one hand to the work, and one prepared for battle. The burden carriers also kept their swords at hand. Our sword is the Word of God. Back to the Ephesians verses: "For we do not wrestle against flesh and blood, but against principalities, against powers, against the rulers of the darkness of this age, against spiritual hosts of wickedness in the heavenly places" (Ephesians 6:12). We, too, must live with our Sword at the ready.

What did it take for the enemies of God's people to turn away? How does this encourage, comfort, or inspire you?

What were the results of Nehemiah's splitting the workforce into workers and armed defense?

How do we armor up today? How does this benefit us?

Against whom is our battle, according to Ephesians 6:12?

Jesus met Satan's temptations in the desert with the Word of God (Luke 4:1–13). Since he was brazenly bold enough to tempt Jesus, God incarnate, Satan will undoubtedly try to tempt the most pious Christian. However, how we carry our Sword, the Word of God, will determine the length of his stay. Therefore, we must be in the Word.

Read 2 Timothy 3:16–17. What did Paul tell us about the value of Scripture? Write the points.

According to Luke 4:13, what did Satan do when his effort to tempt Jesus failed?

Review 1 Peter 5:8. In light of this section of Nehemiah and the above verses, what do these enemy tactics look like today?

Satan might go away as you draw on your trusty sword, standing confident in your armor and position in Christ, but he will keep watch. He will look for a disappointment, an offense, or even a lack of sleep for an opportunity to pounce. He will not waste his opportunities. It is up to us to make sure he has fewer and fewer. Take some time to sit with the Lord and ask Him where your armor needs strengthening. Ask Him to show you how to do it. He will. Wait, believing He wants to speak with you. His desire is for your best. He is not waiting for an opportunity to show you where you lack. He is waiting for permission to make you more awesome than you already are—in Him.

The enemy will go away and wait for an opportune time. For what is he looking?

What can you do specifically this week to rob Satan of opportunities in your life?

For what is God waiting? Do you live like you believe this? If not, why not? How might your life look different if you did believe this fully?

DAY FIVE

NEHEMIAH 4:18–23

What did every builder have in verse 18? If this correlates to the Word of God in your life, how would you apply this spiritually?

Who was beside Nehemiah? What was his role? How might this have comforted the workers?

What else jumps out at you as you read these verses? (What are your observations?)

Nehemiah armed, positioned, encouraged, and got the people back to kingdom business. Then he set one more plan to wisely prepare for an attack and give those under his care courage and a sense of safety. He had the one who sounded the trumpet on call right beside him. He would keep watch, and the trumpeter would call attention to any place of danger.

This would free the workers to focus on their work. Though they carried their weapons prepared for battle, knowing someone was watching over them with a trumpet to alert them had to give them confidence. It is a great feeling to work in service of the kingdom, knowing someone has your back; someone is watching over you to protect, encourage, and release you to your call. Volunteers, in particular, can serve with more commitment, care, and excellence when they know they are being watched over by those they serve. It is essential to pray for our leaders and our leaders for us.

I will never forget the pastor of the megachurch I attended. He was the most shining example of what a pastor ought to be that I have ever experienced. One day, as a volunteer greeter handing out bulletins, I was scheduled to serve at the door through which the pastor entered the sanctuary. I had been greeting for years before being assigned to this most coveted position. Most of the congregation would never meet the senior pastor one-on-one in this large church.

He entered the sanctuary, and I suddenly was unsure if I was supposed to give him a bulletin or not—awkward. He stopped, turned to me with the love and light of Christ in his eyes, and asked how I was. He meant it. He did not ask in passing. He stopped—and loved me. As a volunteer, it was a beautiful moment. I was seen and acknowledged in such a gracious way.

People make up God's kingdom. Some are professional Christians, and others are not. Some are rich, some poor. Some are well-educated, and others are not. People from all walks of life and different backgrounds make up the body of Christ. Some have been in church their whole lives, and others are just beginning to know the joys of life in Christ. All are God's children. All stand on equal ground at the foot of the Cross.

It is time for the church to lay aside roles, culture, and traditions to practice loving each other passionately with the love of Christ. It is time to lay aside the spirits of jealousy, competition, and everything leading to social stratification within the church.

We all matter; we all belong; we are all worthy of mutual care and compassion (Romans 12:10). I say this knowing I am also part of the Church. I point no fingers at anyone. We are all being sanctified and growing in Christ daily. We are each at different places in our spiritual growth, so we must pick up patience and extend grace to each other as we mature. We cannot expect perfection from anyone but Jesus; to all others, grace and patience, wrapped in humility.

What else did Nehemiah set in place, and how would it affect the workers?

What is it time for the church to lay aside? What is it time to pick up?

What do you need to lay down or pick up as a member of the body of Christ today?

NEHEMIAH 4:19–23

Nehemiah acknowledged the immensity of the project. He did not shame or manipulate; he stated the facts as they were. It *was* a big job; there was a lot more wall than there were people (Nehemiah 4:19). His encouragement was speaking in terms of their reality, setting a plan, and getting everyone on the same plan. It must have instilled confidence in his ability to lead, care for, and protect the workers. He planned for everyone to drop their work and run to the trumpet blast, should there be one. They would defend and care for one another. They would trust their leader and build trust in one another while gaining a sense of ownership in the project and the community.

Finally, when the plans were in place, Nehemiah finished with, "Our God will fight for us" (Nehemiah 4:20). It was a good reminder for the congregation of workers, these children of God. No matter how much planning, grit, or purpose they put into the plan, God would ultimately bring victory. Here is the beautiful balance of our responsibility versus God's. We must put on all of our armor, walk with Him in obedience, and trust Him. We do not bear the responsibility for the outcome. We have only to trust and obey.

Nehemiah made another decision, and it protected the workers physically and mentally. We back up to the statements made by those who lived in the outlying areas near the enemies of Jerusalem and Nehemiah's work. They came to Jerusalem and repeated the rumors and threats of their enemies. Nehemiah wisely decided to have everyone stay in Jerusalem for the remainder of the work. It would keep the weak and fearful safe from enemy intimidation and protect them physically.

Scripture tells us they did not change out of their clothes for sleep. Instead, they worked, stood guard, and remained battle-ready day and night. They were committed to the cause and would not let these God-haters disrupt God's plans for them and His kingdom. It is a physical representation of a spiritual truth Peter shares with us in his letter.

Look up 2 Peter 1:10. What does Peter encourage us to do, and what is the promise?

What did Nehemiah acknowledge? How was this a wise move?

How was having a plan and bringing everyone in on the agenda beneficial to the workers? How have you experienced this at home, work, church, or other places? How did it make you feel?

What is the beautiful balance of our responsibility versus God's? How are you encouraged by this truth?

Why was Nehemiah's decision to have everyone stay in Jerusalem wise? How might we see this work today?

What had brought them thus far? Commitment and perseverance in the Lord's call. What has God called you to do that seems insurmountable? Are you sure it is your call? If yes, what stops you from picking up the first stone and placing it on the wall? Nehemiah's wall did not miraculously appear. They built it with good leadership, wisdom, cooperation, and one stone at a time. There were issues along the way, and they prayed, made a plan, and adjusted. What can you do this week to move forward or get back on track? Will you commit right now to armor up, make a plan, and choose to pick up one stone at a time? If you do this, pretty soon, you will be flourishing. Just take the next courageous step in faith and watch God show up to bless your efforts.

Nehemiah Confronts Injustice

WEEK EIGHT / DAY ONE

Nehemiah 5:1–6:19

NEHEMIAH 5:1–5

What about Nehemiah's character and leadership might have sparked hope in the people?

How have you seen this in the leaders in your life? In your leadership? Why is this a critical leadership quality?

What reason did the Israelites have to cry out to Nehemiah for help?

When did they bring their issues to him? Why might they have thought he was the person they could trust with their concern?

Nehemiah's workers and fellow Israelites had been staying in Jerusalem, working long shifts during the day to rebuild the wall and guarding the city by night. They were giving all they had to Nehemiah's cause. It was their cause, but Nehemiah carried the calling and authority. Though their work was hard, it was also spiritually profound. They were building for Nehemiah, for themselves and their families, for their countrymen, and for God. The work was exhausting, the stress of enemy awareness was taxing, and they must have had moments of feeling very overwhelmed.

These Israelites were becoming familiar with Nehemiah's leadership style. They had seen him care for the wall of Jerusalem and deal with both foreign and domestic people. His integrity as a leader probably sparked hope, and they cried out against the oppression they were suffering (Nehemiah 5:1).

The people and their wives protested against unjust treatment by their own people (Nehemiah 5:1). They were not complaining about the hard work or their enemies' tactics. They were calling attention to the oppressive behavior of their brethren. They were struggling financially due to a famine. They had mortgaged properties, sold children into slavery, and borrowed money to pay their taxes. The Israelites they had borrowed from charged interest they could not pay. They were in dire circumstances when Nehemiah arrived.

Look up Exodus 22:25 and Deuteronomy 23:19–20 and note why these borrowers would have a reason to cry out to Nehemiah against their brethren.

According to Leviticus 25:10, what safety net did God provide the Israelites in the Law to protect their inheritance in the event of poor investments?

What do we have today in the United States based on this system?

God's purpose in Jubilee was to restore and redeem those who made poor decisions or ruined investment returns (Leviticus 25:10). Our current bankruptcy system comes from this principle. God also provided the Israelites with the law of the kinsman-redeemer, who could purchase back persons and lands (Leviticus 25:25). Nehemiah's workers' unfortunate circumstances meant they could not redeem anyone or anything because they had mortgaged their lands. They had no money left to redeem their children from slavery. What dismal circumstances, indeed. The Israelites had allowed more than the wall to break down.

We see they did not bring the issue to Nehemiah until it was a desperate situation and came as a cry of distress. They had known they were in trouble when they took their first loan and agreed to pay interest. Their situation soon spiraled out of control, but they did not say anything until this time. Nehemiah's integrity in leadership likely gave them hope enough to publicize their anguish.

We do not have to wait for our problems to become crises before we deal with them. We cannot expect others, especially those in authority over us, to know everything about our circumstances. We also cannot expect our spouse or other family members to know what is bothering us, no matter how obvious it seems. If we genuinely want to reach a resolution, we must learn to verbalize our struggles before we are overcome with emotion. What is most important is to approach with a heart to reconcile. When we adopt a victim's mentality or a need to win, we seek justification, not reconciliation.

I used my inheritance money in my early twenties to attend a vocational school. I ran out of money a couple of months before I ran out of school and found I could not make my car payment. I was devastated. I thought I would lose everything, including the excellent credit I had built. Instead of burying my head and hoping it would disappear, I called the bank. They were very gracious and worked with me. The call saved my credit and my car. If fear of what could go wrong had prevented me from bringing the problem to the one who could fix it, everything would have gone wrong.

Hopefully, all matters are well with you as you read this today. But if not, what will you do about it? Will you ask God to help you get outside of the emotion and give you wisdom and words to bring it to the attention of the right person? Approach it with honesty and humility. The Lord will be with you to help you through your difficult situations. It does not mean that if you do every bit right, the other person will, too. It does mean you have treated a circumstance with biblical integrity, and God will give you favor regardless. Trust Him with the process.

What must we learn to do when we want to find a solution to our problems? Why is this necessary?

What goal should motivate us when we bring an issue to the table? What sort of conclusion are we seeking? For what are we not looking?

How can you know if you are seeking reconciliation or justification?

Why is it essential to approach a challenging situation with honesty and humility?

Are you guaranteed to receive the same integrity you give? What can you find comfort in when this happens?

NEHEMIAH 5: 6–9

Nehemiah heard these complaints of injustice and oppression between Israelites and was angry. Of course he was! Nehemiah was not a truly free man. He was still the king's servant-friend. He lived tethered to his lord and master, and these Israelites were, at the very least, free to live in their own land. Nehemiah was obligated to return to Persia upon completion of the job, they would get to remain in Jerusalem. Nehemiah learned his countrymen were using and abusing their relationships, taking their positions, blessings, and connections for granted.

In chapter one, we saw Nehemiah's care and concern for his brethren in Jerusalem and his desire to know the state of affairs there. He longed to be there, to build this wall, and to make a safe place for his brethren to dwell together; he must have imagined a remnant of God's people living and working together. He may have thought they would support one another as enemies surrounded them.

He was utterly disappointed to find them devouring one another financially. Enemy forces were confronting Nehemiah, seeking to kill, steal, and destroy his dream and call to see Jerusalem's wall rebuilt. The homeland he had been dreaming of and praying for with deep concern and passion was now a great disappointment.

Yes; Nehemiah was angry, but he did not sin. We learn he gave serious thought to the matter before responding. Nehemiah did not react out of his emotions. Instead, he took time to consider. He was about to address those who held financial and political power. It would be wise to consider his response carefully. Rebuking one's peers, leaders, or the powerful must be preceded by significant thought and humble prayer.

How did Nehemiah react to the people's complaints? Is this an appropriate response? Why or why not?

What did Nehemiah find disappointing? What disappoints you about church family? (Do not be too specific or use names if you share this in a group.)

Nehemiah was angry but did not sin. What did he do before he addressed the group? Why was this so important?

When Nehemiah was ready, he confronted them with the simple truth, "Each of you is exacting usury from his brother" (Nehemiah 5:7). These brethren of Nehemiah knew better. Yet they were letting their kin sell their own children into slavery to cover their debts. The nobles and rulers could only respond to Nehemiah with complete silence. The truth tends to have this effect on injustice; it illuminates dark places. Isaiah prophesied, "Every valley shall be exalted and every mountain and hill brought low; the crooked places shall be made straight and the rough places smooth" (Isaiah 40:4). Truth levels, straightens, and silences corruption.

Nehemiah exposed the nobles and rulers as men who did not fear God because their actions were corrupt. Where the fear of God is absent, violence is near. These men committed violence against their countrymen's families and livelihoods. Fear of God in this context means respect, reverence, and awe of God. It means one would not easily defy Him because one would not desire to dishonor Him.

Nehemiah also told the nobles and rulers they should be concerned over the reproach of their enemies because of their actions. Paul's second letter to the Corinthian church tells us we are ambassadors of Christ (2 Corinthians 5:20). We are His representation on the earth. We know from Matthew 28:16–18 we are called to make disciples of all nations. Our business here on earth is to be fishers of men. We can only do this if we are behaving in ways consistent with the Cross of Christ. When our actions repel the lost, we are no different from those Nehemiah was rebuking here. We find ourselves in these places when we lose reverence for our Holy God. He is both a consuming fire and a loving father (Hebrews 12:29; John 3:16). Our perfect response is to live with love, honor, and awe as His children, considering how we represent our Father to a lost and broken world.

What does John 13:35 say about our witness to the world?

It is impressive to see how the Israelites worked side by side to build the wall, keep watch, and stand battle ready with and for one another, regardless of the turmoil in their relationships. Kingdom building can still progress even when we are not getting all our relationships right in the body. Why? Because God is bigger than all of it. I have learned this phrase over the past few years as I have walked through several fiery trials. I can either collapse into a puddle of sweat and tears or realize God is bigger than all of it and place my trust in Him. He helps me understand that my mountains are molehills in His sight. They are neither a problem nor a surprise for Him, but they invite me to learn how to lean into Him when my world seems controlled by chaos.

With what did Nehemiah confront the truth? Why might this approach be a good choice in this circumstance?

What effect did Nehemiah's approach have on those he confronted? Why was this an appropriate response?

What is it to have the fear of God? What happens when the fear of God is absent?

Why should they and we be concerned about the reproach of our enemies?

Why can kingdom building continue when inner turmoil is present? How does this encourage you today?

We see mountains; God sees molehills. What are we invited to do in the face of our mountains?

DAY TWO

NEHEMIAH 5:10–13

What did Nehemiah confess? How was this a problem?

What did Nehemiah say needed to be done? How did they respond?

Once Nehemiah stated the truth and rebuked the leaders, he confessed he, too, had been lending to the people. He was unaware of the situation and was showing compassionate leadership toward a hardworking but struggling group of Israelites. So he lent, not knowing the dire situation they would all be in if he did not immediately correct their course.

He first charged them to stop exacting interest on the loans. The New King James Version (NKJV) translates it as, "Please, let us stop," but God's Word Translation (GW) says, "We must stop." Several translate the phrase "leave off." The intent is clear; I do not think Nehemiah was making a polite request, as in, "Please, will you do this?" It seems more likely that it was emphatic, as GW has translated it. Nehemiah then directed all the lenders to restore all collateral for all loans: lands, vineyards, olive groves, houses, a hundredth of their money and grain, the new wine, and the oil (Nehemiah 5:11). No wonder they cried out to Nehemiah in distress—what did they have left?

The beautiful surprise was that they agreed to do as Nehemiah requested. The wise surprise was Nehemiah's calling the priests to get the Israelites' word in an ordained oath. They were living as though God was not able to see their sin. Nehemiah shrewdly called the priests to remind these upper-class lenders of their relationship with God. It would be more difficult to break their oath to God than to Nehemiah, the mere mortal who would go back to Persia one day.

How had the upper-class lenders been living? What did involving the priests accomplish for Nehemiah and the Israelites?

Are you living your life as though God is present at all times? Where might you be compartmentalizing your life? How can you use the example above to restore relationship to those areas?

Why is God in relationship with you? What is He not in relationship with you to do?

Here is a good moment to do a self-check. It is an excellent question to ask ourselves often. Am I living as though God is always present—all-seeing, all-knowing—or am I compartmentalizing my life? Is God welcome in all aspects of my life or just the ones where I think I can please Him? Is He invited to help pick movies, games, friends, and menus? It is easier when we remember He is in it for the relationship because He loves us. He is not in it to police our activities but to participate in life with us. Take some time to ask Him to show you just one area of your life He would like more access to, then look forward to enjoying the adventure of including Him. Record your thoughts below.

NEHEMIAH 5:14–19

Chapter five finishes with a compare-and-contrast. Nehemiah spoke another truth, this one about his leadership as governor. He was appointed governor and said that for twelve years, neither he nor his companions ate the governor's portions. Nevertheless, Nehemiah led with a generous spirit, not even taking what was his to have. Nehemiah demonstrates the balance between receiving with gratitude the blessings God has provided and holding them loosely. God's generosity remains a blessing when it does not become an entitlement. Nehemiah chose to share his blessing; he had enough without adding to the burden of the people he had come to serve. Nehemiah pointed out how his predecessors had taken advantage of this perk of the office. He, however, did not "because of the fear of God" (Nehemiah 5:15).

Read Matthew 20:25–28. What did Jesus say to His disciples about leadership? How does this show in your life/ministry?

Read Luke 12:30–32 and note what it says about provision. Do you live like this is true?

God gets the credit for Nehemiah's position, as he demonstrates the concept Jesus taught hundreds of years later. The work continued on the wall even amid these external and internal crises. Meals were served with an abundance of provisions, even though Nehemiah declined the benefits of his office. What an excellent example: We do not have to grasp for our blessings. God will provide for all our needs. It is His good pleasure to care for us. The advice of Jesus is simple: seek His kingdom first. Nehemiah shows us how to live this out.

How did Nehemiah's leadership compare and contrast with his predecessors? What lessons can you glean and apply to your own life?

What blessings do you see in Nehemiah's not demanding the benefits of his office as governor?

What helps the gifts of God remain blessings in our lives?

Is there an area where you struggle with seeking His kingdom first and trusting Him with the timing and provision? How might you be encouraged by Nehemiah's example?

What is your Father's good pleasure?

Nehemiah concluded this chapter by stepping out of narration and writing his heartfelt words directly to the Father. Write those words below from verse 19.

Nehemiah's prayer might seem out of place alongside Nehemiah's generous and compassionate leadership style, so it requires a closer look. We have just seen that Nehemiah was not seeking temporal benefits from those he served. Here, we see he desired no reward other than what comes from heaven.

Nehemiah asked God to remember him for good. The Bible uses the word *remember* two hundred thirty-one times. Often, it represents seeking or acknowledging God's favor. Sometimes, it seeks a return from God—a kindness for good deeds done, if you will. For example, when Jesus was on the cross, one of the thieves said to Him, "Remember me when You come into Your kingdom" (Luke 23:42). He sought to have his name written in the Lamb's Book of Life.

This word *remember* can, by implication, mean "to mention," which furthers the thought of the previous paragraph. Where would Jesus "mention" him?

Read Matthew 10:32 and Revelation 3:5. Where will Jesus mention your name? What is required for Him to speak your name there? How is this demonstrated in your life?

Finally, Nehemiah said, "Remember me for good." We can agree it is good to have Jesus speak our names before the Father and write them in His heavenly book. However, God's provision and protection allow us to enjoy terrestrial goodness. Nehemiah sought God for his earthly welfare, prosperity, and happiness. We can see he did not engage the Lord in this request to spend it on himself but to continue the generous and compassionate lifestyle he would like to continue.

Read James 4:3. What does James point out as a hindrance to answered prayers?

Nehemiah had already shown he did not ask in order to spend toward his own pleasure but to spend himself for others. What an excellent example of leadership. He must have been exhausted; no wonder he sought God to remember him for good, including happiness. It only took fifty-two days to build the wall. In those days, he had dealt with troubles from outside and in. He just came to rebuild a wall, but in doing so, he found himself also rebuilding a people and a way of life. He could not have accomplished this remarkable feat without his great God.

For what did Nehemiah want God to remember him?

What are the terrestrial benefits of God's goodness?

Was it okay for Nehemiah to make this request of God? Why or why not?

What was Nehemiah building?

Does Nehemiah inspire you to change the way you pray? How will you employ those gifts for the kingdom? Be specific.

How does knowing God's eyes are on you for good make you feel? Do you shrink away from the thought or press into the truth? Ask Him to expand your ability to comprehend His goodness toward you today.

In what area are you asking God to remember you for good today? Did you know you could ask Him for favor and blessings? As seen with Nehemiah, the key is to ask for kingdom purposes, not to spend it on yourself. Ask Him to broaden your thinking about kingdom building today. Ask Him to give you a mindset to ask for more than you can think or imagine, then watch and see what He will do because His eyes are on you for good. Write a prayer here.

DAY THREE

NEHEMIAH 6:1–9

What was the core purpose of Nehemiah's enemies' attacks?

Where did they direct their next attack when they were not ready to admit defeat? How did they seek to stop the work at this point?

How did Nehemiah respond to this attempt to pull him away from his work? What did he know about his work that kept him focused?

What is one often-used tactic of the enemy? What are some ways you combat this attack?

What was the message in the open letter? Have you ever had a similar experience? How did you handle it?

What were the rumors attacking? What was their purpose? How did Nehemiah respond, and how is this an example for you?

How did Nehemiah's assessment of the enemy's plan and purpose help him know how to pray?

In chapter six, we meet with Nehemiah as his passion comes to fruition. He began in Persia as the king's servant-friend, far from where his heart was attached. He longed to know the state of his people in Jerusalem. Finally, Nehemiah completed the wall except for the doors and gates. Seeing this project so close to completion must have felt good. Still, though the finish was in sight, he could not yet sigh relief at a well-done job. His enemies were not giving up their fight against Jerusalem and God's people.

Based on verse 1, our regular players Sanballat, Tobiah, and Geshem heard of Nehemiah's success in building the wall. They had tried many intimidation tactics throughout the building process, but they seemed to have learned nothing. They were not ready to admit defeat. Sanballat and Geshem escalated their defiance. They had gone after his character by spreading rumors, planned attacks, and attempted to undermine his work through various means. This time, instead of bringing the fight to Nehemiah, they tried to draw Nehemiah away from the work and the safety of the wall he had just built. They sent to call him out to meet them in the plain of Ono, which was located twenty-five to thirty miles from Jerusalem.[i]

Nehemiah did not allow them to distract him from his purpose. He knew who and how they were. They had made it clear from the beginning. If their intentions were friendship, they would have come to him. He wisely declined their invitation, emphasizing the essential nature of his work, which required his presence. The text does not mention that he prayed over this. Sometimes, we know the correct response; we do not need to twist our minds up with the possibilities. At other times we need to assess the value of an invitation and whether it merits leaving our current focus.

Whenever I need to focus on studying, writing, or a kingdom deadline, I begin to receive many calls and texts. I have learned it is okay to let calls go to voicemail when I know the Lord has given me a directive. I can respond to texts later. Any new business could be an intentional distraction to draw me away. One often-used tactic of our enemy is distraction. We must learn to discern the difference between distraction and legitimate interruptions, just as Nehemiah did here. If the enemy can get us off task, he has at least delayed the work, if not drawn us away completely. Discern what is worthy of your momentary attention and what is not. Then let go of guilt. God will never guilt you into serving Him.

Finally, Nehemiah's enemies sent him an open letter. His familiarity with the Persian royal court would have caused him to recognize the intent of the open letter. It was a sign of public disrespect. When sending a letter to a person of high regard or position, Persian custom was to seal it and deliver it in a type of purse. Open letters were for non-dignitaries or to express disrespect.[ii] The message was clear. The opposition was telling Nehemiah they did not recognize his authority in their region, and they had no intention of showing him respect. Their vitriol was coming to a crescendo.

Though more direct in its approach, their letter repeated former tactics. They were trying to start rumors about Nehemiah's intentions and integrity. They sought to intimidate Nehemiah by telling him there were claims he wanted to position himself as king and had hired prophets to declare it. They accused him then sought an audience with him. It did not require much discernment to see through this attempt.

Once again, Nehemiah spent little to no time on it. He did not defend himself against the charge or get caught up in a game he was not meant to play. Instead, he remained focused on his purpose and gave the enemy a dose of truth. "No such things as you say are being done, but you invent them in your own heart" (Nehemiah 6:8).

I cannot help but think of Jesus's being tempted in the desert by Satan (Luke 4:1–14). To every temptation, Jesus responded with Scripture—truth. Nehemiah, while not quoting Scripture, did succinctly speak the truth, and it was the end of the letter writing. When the devil was finished tempting Jesus, he went away. Nehemiah would stand firm, and these enemies would fade away, too. However, we still study Nehemiah today to learn tactics to combat the enemy's wiles.

Nehemiah prayed to his God at this point. He acknowledged the problem: "They all were trying to make us afraid" (Nehemiah 6:9). He asked God to provide the opposite of what the enemy planned for them. The enemy planned weakness, so Nehemiah prayed for strength (Nehemiah 6:9).

How would you spiritualize Nehemiah's completed wall—except for the doors and gates—to represent someone's walk with Jesus? What might the doors and gates represent? Why would this leave someone open to spiritual attacks?

Why did Nehemiah not have to pray to God to find his answer this time? How does this example help or encourage you?

What is one often-used tactic of the enemy? What are some ways you combat this attack?

What did the devil do when he was finished tempting Jesus? What will he do if you stand on truth long enough? What truth must you stand on today to keep the enemy at bay?

Yes, Lord, let every tactic of the enemy backfire by making us better, stronger, and more resilient as we seek to serve Your kingdom. Let us not be distracted by lies, rumors, or any other tactic the enemy throws at us. Let us, instead, look to truth, trust You, and rely on You. Help us keep our eyes and minds focused with great resolve on what You have placed before us to do. "The simple believes every word, but the prudent considers well his steps" (Proverbs 14:15).

DAY FOUR

NEHEMIAH 6:10–16

Nehemiah's enemies employed one more tactic. Through whom did they attack Nehemiah? Who was he to Nehemiah?

The former attack was direct and public. What was different about this attack?

Nehemiah overcame his enemies' attempts to draw him away from his work. He withstood their public attack on his character, knowing their lies had no merit. He prayed and continued the work, but his enemies were tenacious. They would employ one more tactic. As long as the doors and gates remained unfinished, they would not let up until the workers cut off all access.

This is where we meet Nehemiah's friend, Shemaiah. His name means "heard by Jah."[iii] He was a Merarite Levite.[iv] Shemaiah was a Levite, the son of a priest, an intimate and confidential friend of Nehemiah, and claimed to be a prophet, but Nehemiah's enemies secretly bribed him.[v] His father's name was Delaiah, and his name meant "Jah has drawn."[vi] His grandfather was Mehetabeel, which means "favored of God."[vii]

First, according to the information above and in light of the tactics of the enemy, we see the attack move from a direct, public attack to a personal, private attack. This close friend turned against Nehemiah for an undisclosed sum of money. Our enemy will try to use those closest to us to do us harm or instill fear. It is essential to understand this. Who better to get under our skin than someone we trust and hold dear? We should understand the enemy's ability to manipulate those we love to work against us on his behalf, and he also has the potential to influence us to do the same. This is why it is vital to remain in Jesus and He in us (John 15:4). We must be daily in His Word and experience an ongoing, surrendered relationship with Him. It is the best way to grow in our ability to discern truth from lies and learn to sense Holy Spirit warnings.

Why would the enemy attempt to use someone close to us?

Why is it important to note our enemy's ability to use our loved ones against us?

What can you do to be able to discern the enemy's tactics?

Another point to recognize is that though this man's name was "Heard By God," it does not mean he was hearing God. Though he claimed to be a prophet, it did not mean he was a prophet. Most often, prophets do not have to advertise. Their correct words will advertise for them. We should always judge by fruit and not by words. If the prophet's life reveals the fruit of Christ and his or her words prove true, we can agree they at least possess a prophetic gift, if not of the office of prophet (Ephesians 4:11).

We also see that being descended from a line of priests, even assuming they were faithful followers, did not guarantee the man named Heard By God would become faithful, too. We cannot carry our parents' faith, and our children cannot carry ours. We each must come to our own real and personal relationship with Jesus. We must know Him for ourselves. We must move from religion to personal experience and relationship with Him. Nehemiah has been showing the difference and how it ought to look. He is about to do it again.

Shemaiah was a priest and a prophet. What does this tell you about following someone based on a title? What should you do?

How do we move from religion to relationship?

Nehemiah went to his friend's home, where his friend told him his enemies were coming to kill him. His intimate friend suggested they go together to the temple and lock themselves in for safety. On the surface, this seems like a nice offer. Sadly, Nehemiah's friend offered to bring him into the holy of holies.[viii] This was the innermost part of the sanctuary, where only priests could go. It was an appeal to Nehemiah's pride of office and an invitation for Nehemiah to sin against God. How sad.

Nehemiah, a man whose heart truly belonged to his God, was not inclined toward this appeal to his pride. He refused quickly and adamantly. Nehemiah would not use his office to extract special favors from man or God—especially not God. Nehemiah knew from where his blessings flowed. He had repeatedly seen God protect his integrity on this wall-building journey. His friend tempted him to hide in the inner room of a temple, surrounded by the temple walls and the wall of Jerusalem. It was a temptation to discount the work done on the wall, suggesting his effort would not be enough. Yet it was.

God will extend your sphere of influence. The enemy will immediately attempt to intimidate you to shrink to a smaller sphere than God has ordained. Just like Nehemiah, we need to reach for the outer limits of what God has ordained for us. We must learn to fill the space He has afforded us instead of hiding ourselves in the safe inner sanctuary. How do we do it? Look at Nehemiah. He found a passion and reached beyond what he thought possible, and the doors flung wide open before him. Then, he stayed faithful to the task in the face of every obstacle and threat. He proved God over and over, and he filled the space given to him by God through prayer, faith, and commitment.

Nehemiah discerned the false prophecy at the point of his humble refusal to abuse his privilege. Isn't this interesting? He knew what was right. He did not pray and ask God to show him the way; he chose the way he knew was right, then God revealed the plot. Again, his enemies sought to cause Nehemiah to sin against his God so they could have tangible evidence against him, this time for his people.

Nehemiah's appropriate response was to pray and ask God to remember his enemies. Not long ago, Nehemiah had asked God to remember him for his deeds, which were good. Here, he asked God to remember these men who had harassed him from the moment his purpose was made public. They tried many tactics to stop Nehemiah from fulfilling his call. Nehemiah asked God to remember them for it. When Nehemiah had asked God to remember him, he asked for God's provision and protection upon him. This time, he asked God to remove provision and protection from his enemies, based on their work against Him. Nehemiah was asking God to thwart every tactic brought against kingdom work.

What was wrong with Nehemiah's friend's offer? Why?

How did Nehemiah refuse his friend? How is this an example in today's polite society?

What foundation helped Nehemiah come to his swift decision to refuse his friend?

What does the enemy attempt to convince you of regarding your sphere of influence? What do you need to do? Where is that sphere for you?

How did Nehemiah fill the space given to him? How have you emulated this in your own life?

What happened when Nehemiah chose the way he knew was right? What was the enemy's purpose in this ploy?

What did Nehemiah pray and ask God to do? How does this compare/contrast with Nehemiah's prayer when he asked God to remember him?

I am so grateful God does not remember my evil works before I came to Him in truth and repentance. I was reminded of the following verses as I wrote the previous paragraph. Write them below.

Psalms 103:12

Isaiah 43:25

Years ago, I attended Bible Study Fellowship as a new believer and had an excellent Bible teacher. She said, when we confess and repent of sin we have already confessed and repented of, God says, "When did you do that? I do not remember you ever doing that." This is how far east is from west.

Aren't you grateful to find complete forgiveness in Christ, no matter how sinful your past might be? Moreover, his memory of us transforms in the process. Previously, He saw our sin, but now, in Christ, He looks toward us for our protection, provision, and much more. Indeed, "If God is for us, who can be against us" (Romans 8:31b)?

By the way, Nehemiah finished the wall in a miraculous fifty-two days! For reference, if you have followed this study week by week and did only five lessons per week, day fifty-two fell on day three of week eight—yesterday! Can you imagine building the physical wall of Jerusalem in this time frame, with enemies constantly harassing you? How much greater is the ability to repair and create healthy spiritual, physical, and emotional boundaries as we study Nehemiah's wall?

Nehemiah finished the work in an extraordinarily short amount of time. Considering the job before them, the state of the people when he came, and all the tactics of the enemy thrown at them, we can truly see what it looks like when God remembers us for good. We faithfully move forward when we set our hearts and minds on Him and whatever He has placed before us. He miraculously brings it to fruition better than we could have imagined. So go ahead, shout some praise!

How far is your sin removed from you? Do you fully believe that? How do you respond to the thought of God's forgetting the sins you have already repented of? Do you walk in this truth today?

How are we now remembered in Christ?

How long did it take for Nehemiah's wall to be finished? Why is this a notable miracle?

What happens when we faithfully move forward for kingdom business? Can you share a time when you experienced this?

DAY FIVE

NEHEMIAH 6:17–19

In the final few verses of this chapter, we discover why Tobiah had been so bold in his harassment of Nehemiah. In these verses, we learn that two Jewish families had made unholy alliances with Tobiah through his and his son's marriages. Later chapters in Nehemiah deal with the Isrraelites' intermarrying with those who were not Jewish—one of the very sins that had caused their exile in the first place. It was against the Mosaic Law to intermarry with other nations (Deuteronomy 7:4; 2 Corinthians 6:14). The exception was when those foreigners renounced their origins to become Israelites in culture and religion. The Book of Ruth gives us one example in Ruth the Moabitess. She renounced her father's gods, returned to Israel with her mother-in-law, Naomi, and committed to Naomi's God and country. She became the wife of Boaz and great-grandmother to King David.

We also learn that Tobiah and his son made alliances with people considered nobles (Nehemiah 6:17). Many in Judah had sworn allegiance to Tobiah. It is unclear if this concerns his marriage covenant or another covenant. However, we did learn earlier how the nobles were lending to Israelites at interest, taking their lands, and causing them to sell their children into slavery.

While Tobiah married into Israel, he did not become an Israelite. He had not renounced his gods or his country of origin. Our first introduction to Tobiah in Scripture was as an Ammonite. This title follows him through the book, suggesting he never renounced his former allegiances. He was an enemy of Israel, insinuating himself into the company of Judah's upper classes and religious elites. Then he used those relationships to intimidate Nehemiah further.

We want to glean from this section on Tobiah, for one, that it does not matter with whom our enemy allies himself. Jesus is the Author and Finisher of our faith, and He will not leave or forsake us (Hebrews 12:1–4). When the enemy comes at us, our best response is to lean into Jesus with honest prayers and trust in His ability and desire to care for us.

Why had Tobiah been so bold in his harassment of Nehemiah?

Why were these alliances inappropriate for Israelites? How do we apply that to dating, marriage, and friendship today?

What thoughts and actions will you take away from this study on Nehemiah's building the wall around Jerusalem?

"Therefore we also, since we are surrounded by so great a cloud of witnesses, let us lay aside every weight and the sin which so easily ensnares us, and let us run with endurance the race that is set before us, looking unto Jesus, the author and finisher of our faith, who for the joy that was set before Him endured the cross, despising the shame, and has sat down at the right hand of the throne of God. For consider Him who endured such hostility from sinners against Himself, lest you become weary and discouraged in your souls" (Hebrews 12:1–3).

Appendix

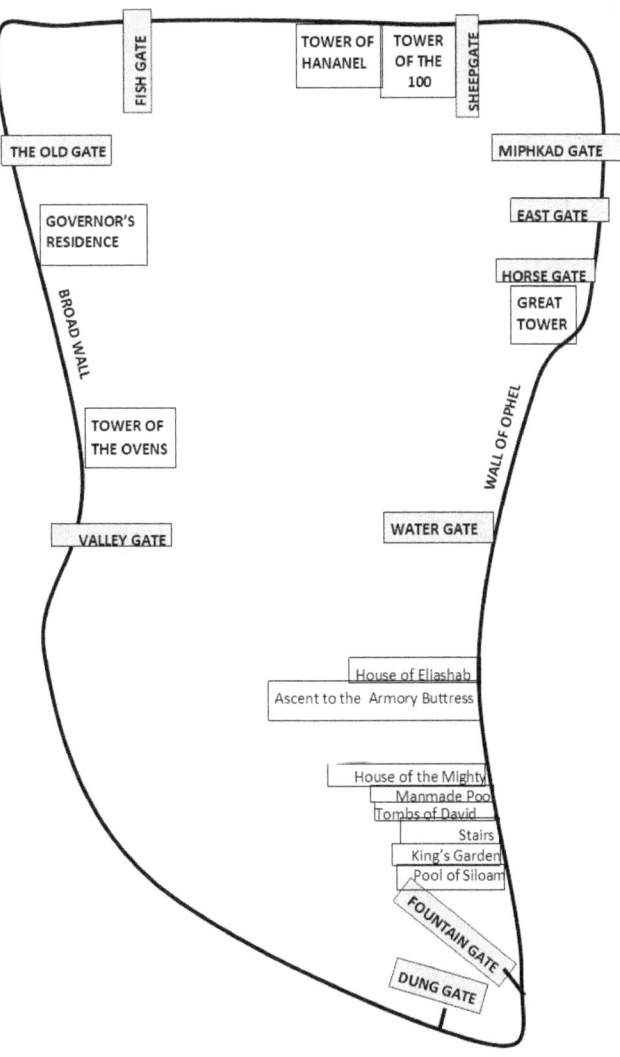

Figure 1: Places on the wall

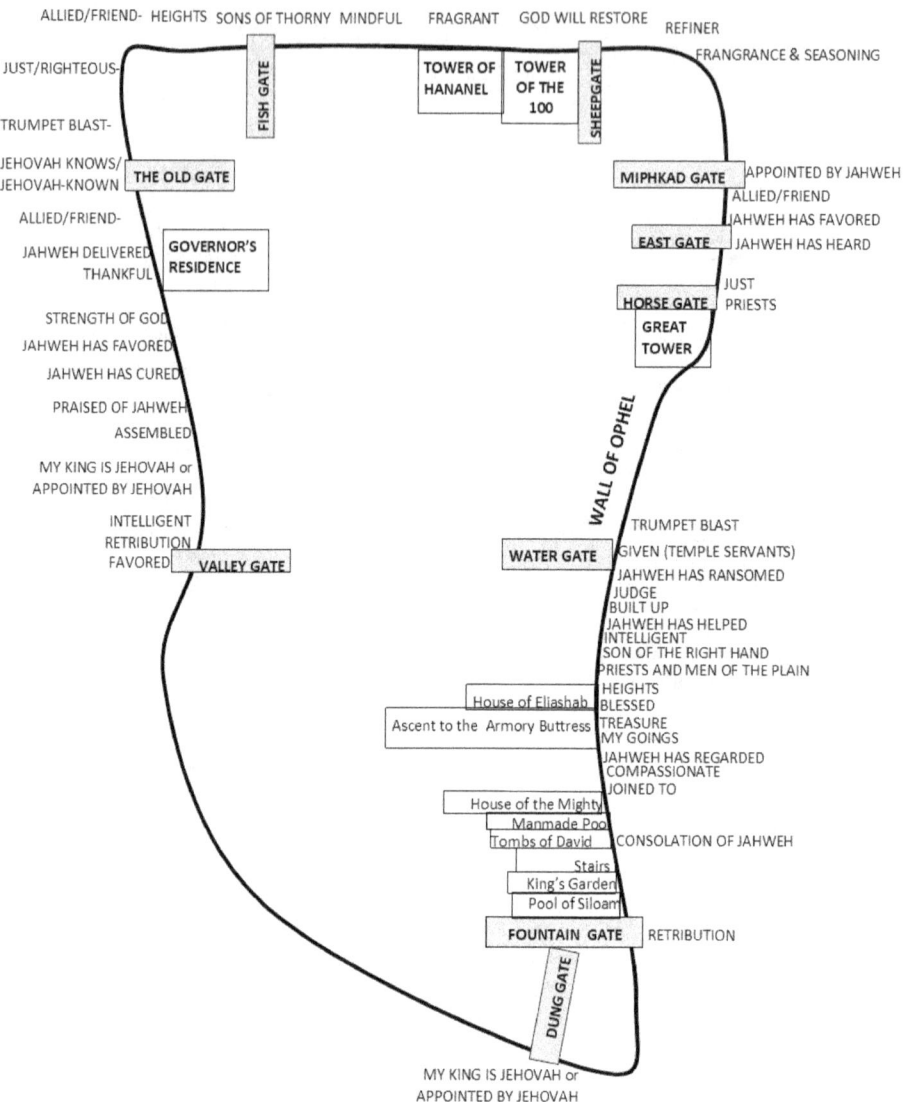

Figure 2: Place and builders with names translated.

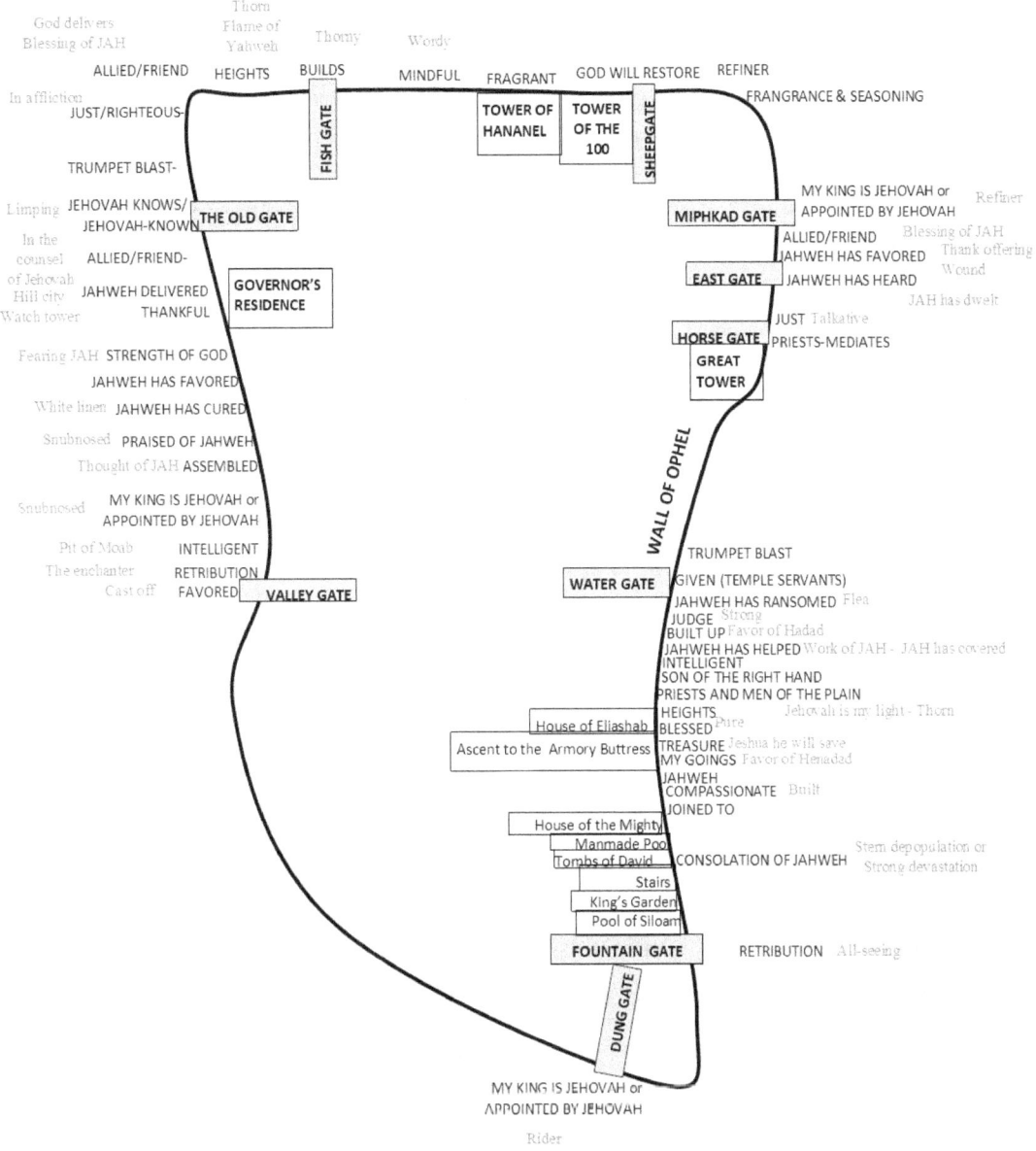

Figure 3: Places, builders, and ancestors; names translated.

About the Author

Jacquie Hoekstra is the author of the highly rated Bible studies *Peter: A Life Transformed* and *Becoming Israel: Jacob's Struggle*. She has also published a short story, *This Servant's Hands*.

Jacquie's thirty years of experience leading groups, Bible studies, and other ministries shine through her written works. She teaches with humor and authenticity. Her journey with inner healing and overcoming trials makes her studies relatable.

Jacquie has degrees in Bible study from Life Pacific College and theology from Canyon College. She was ordained by The International Church of the Foursquare Gospel in 2008. Although she does not currently serve in an official appointment, she continues to preach, teach, and serve on her church's inner healing team.

Jacquie's last move placed her in Brownsville, Oregon, a small historic town famous for two things: It was the filming site of the movie "Stand By Me," and it is in the grass-seed capital of the world. Jacquie enjoys taking in the ever-changing views of the farmlands and watching lambs and calves frolic in the fields. She often spies bald eagles and other birds of prey. The air is fresh, and the pace of life is peaceful.

Jacquie and her husband enjoy their home in the Willamette Valley, between the Cascade Mountains and the Coast Range, surrounded by hazelnut orchards and grass-seed farms. Jacquie especially enjoys watching and photographing sunsets and thanks God daily for these blessings.

Acknowledgments

As I reach the end of this study and think back to the beginning, there are many people to thank. My husband, Martin, has been a constant encourager to me to continue this writing adventure. Thank you, Martin, for being my biggest cheerleader and for your continued support to keep me moving forward. Matt and Anne Spaanem, thank you for always being available and willing to help with anything I ask. You are a treasure to me. Sandy Sturdy, thank you for saving the book cover when I could not figure out the final step. To Nicole Cade, my senior pastor, who always meets my ideas with a resounding "yes" and then supports me in achieving my dreams and goals. To all of my friends who did the study and cheered me on to completion, your time and critiques brought me to the finish line. Finally, a great big thank you to my favorite niece, Anna Cawcutt, for giving your time and expertise to help me finish strong. Each one of you has made this study and writing journey joyful, and you have my deepest gratitude.

Other Books by Jacquie

Endnotes

CHAPTER ONE

i   J. Strong, Strong's Dictionaries, e-Sword Bible study software. e-sword.net.

ii   R. L. Harris, *Theological Wordbook of Old Testament Words* (Chicago: Moody Press, 1980), 854–856.

iii   Harris, Theological Wordbook, 854–856.

iv   Clarke, *Commentary*, e-Sword.

v   J. H. Walton, *The IVP Bible Background Commentary: Old Testament* (Downers Grove, IL: InterVarsity Press, 2000), 472–473.

vi   C. F. Keil and Franz Delitzsch, *Commentary on the Old Testament,* vol. 4 (Peabody, MA, 2011)

vii   Keil and Delitzsch, *Commentary,* 105.

viii   Keil and Delitzsch, *Commentary,* 106.

ix   Walton, The IVP Bible Background, 473.

CHAPTER TWO

i   Harris, Theological Wordbook, 933.

ii   Harris, Theological Wordbook, 933.

iii   Graham Cooke, *Rest Is a Weapon* (Brilliant, Jan. 2017), https://brilliantperspectives.com/rest-is-a-weapon/

iv   J. A. Wenham, *New Bible Commentary* (Leicester, England: InterVarsity Press, 1994), 97.

v   Harris, Theological Wordbook, 159.

vi   R. F. Youngblood, *Nelson's New Illustrated Bible Dictionary* (Nashville: Nelson, 1995), 568.

vii   Harris, Theological Wordbook, 976.

viii   Harris, Theological Wordbook, 663.

ix   Harris, Theological Wordbook, 662.

x   Keil and Delitzsch, *Commentary,* 108.

xi   Harris, Theological Wordbook, 946.

xii   Keil and Delitzsch, *Commentary,* 109.

xiii   F. D. Brown, S. R. Driver, and C. A. Briggs, *The Brown-Driver-Briggs Hebrew and English Lexicon,* (Peabody, MA: Hendrickson, 2003), 744.

xiv   Frank C. Thompson, *The Thompson Chain-Reference Study Bible* (Indianapolis: B. B. Kirkbride Bible Company, 1997), 621, 2214.

xv   Brown, Driver, and Briggs, *Lexicon*, 161.

xvi   Brown, Driver, and Briggs, *Lexicon*, 161.

xvii   Keil and Delitzsch, *Commentary,* 110.

xviii   Keil and Delitzsch, *Commentary,* 108.

xix   Youngblood, *Bible Dictionary*, 1128.

xx   Youngblood, *Bible Dictionary*, 1126.

xxi   Youngblood, *Bible Dictionary*, 1260.

xxii   Keil and Delitzsch, *Commentary,* 108.

xxiii   Wenham, New Bible Commentary, 98.

xxiv   J. Strong, Strong's Hebrew and Greek Dictionaries, e-Sword.

xxv   Wenham, New Bible Commentary, 95.

CHAPTER THREE

i   Strong, *Strong's Dictionaries*, e-Sword.

ii   R. Jamieson, A. R. Fausset, and D. Brown, *Jamieson-Fausset-Brown Bible Commentary*, e-Sword.

iii   Strong, *Strong's Dictionaries*, e-Sword.

iv   Strong, *Strong's Dictionaries*, e-Sword.

v   Strong, *Strong's Dictionaries*, e-Sword.

vi   Strong, *Strong's Dictionaries*, e-Sword.

vii Strong, *Strong's Dictionaries*, e-Sword.

viii Strong, *Strong's Dictionaries*, e-Sword.

ix   Keil and Delitzsch, *Commentary,* 112.

x   Strong, *Strong's Dictionaries*, e-Sword.

xi   Brown, Driver, and Briggs, *Lexicon*, 881.

xii Brown, Driver, and Briggs, *Lexicon*, 1023.

xiii Strong, Strong's Dictionaries, e-Sword.

xiv Strong, *Strong's Dictionaries*, e-Sword.

xv   Strong, *Strong's Dictionaries*, e-Sword. Brown, Driver, and Briggs, *Lexicon,* 842.

xvi Brown, Driver, and Briggs, *Lexicon*, 776.

xvii Brown, Driver, and Briggs, *Lexicon*, e-Sword.

CHAPTER FOUR

i   Brown, Driver, and Briggs, *Lexicon*, 220. Strong, *Strong's Dictionaries*, e-Sword.

ii   Brown, Driver, and Briggs, *Lexicon*, e-Sword. Strong, *Strong's Dictionaries*, e-Sword.

iii   Strong, *Strong's Dictionaries*, e-Sword.

iv   Strong, *Strong's Dictionaries*, e-Sword.

v   Brown, Driver, and Briggs, *Lexicon*, e-Sword.

vi   Brown, Driver, and Briggs, *Lexicon*, 122.

vii Brown, Driver, and Briggs, *Lexicon*, 859.

viii Adam Clarke, Adam Clarke's Commentary on the Bible, e-Sword.

ix   Brown, Driver, and Briggs, *Lexicon*, 739.

x   Strong, *Strong's Dictionaries*, e-Sword.

xi   Strong, *Strong's Dictionaries*, e-Sword.

xii Jamieson, Fausset, and Brown, *Commentary*, e-Sword.

xiii Strong, *Strong's Dictionaries*, e-Sword.

xiv Brown, Driver, and Briggs, *Lexicon*, 301.

xv   Harris, Theological Wordbook, 327.

xvi Strong, *Strong's Dictionaries*, e-Sword.

xvii Brown, Driver, and Briggs, *Lexicon*, 355.

xviii Strong, *Strong's Dictionaries*, e-Sword.

xix Brown, Driver, and Briggs, *Lexicon*, e-Sword. Strong, *Strong's Dictionaries*, e-Sword.

xx   Strong, *Strong's Dictionaries*, e-Sword. Brown, Driver, and Briggs, *Lexicon,* e-Sword.

xxi Strong, *Strong's Dictionaries*, e-Sword.

xxii Strong, *Strong's Dictionaries*, e-Sword.

xxiii Brown, Driver, and Briggs, *Lexicon*, 809, 555.

xxiv Brown, Driver, and Briggs, *Lexicon*, 1024.

xxv Brown, Driver, and Briggs, *Lexicon*, 538.

CHAPTER FIVE

i   Brown, Driver, and Briggs, *Lexicon*, 337.

ii   Strong, *Strong's Dictionaries*, e-Sword.

iii   Strong, *Strong's Dictionaries*, e-Sword.

iv   Brown, Driver, and Briggs, *Lexicon*, 276.

v   Keil and Delitzsch, *Commentary,* 116.

vi   Strong, *Strong's Dictionaries*, e-Sword. Brown, Driver, and Briggs, *Lexicon*, 575.

vii   Strong, *Strong's Dictionaries*, e-Sword.

viii   Strong, *Strong's Dictionaries*, e-Sword.

ix   Brown, Driver, and Briggs, *Lexicon*, 1025.

x   Strong, *Strong's Dictionaries*, e-Sword. Brown, Driver, and Briggs, *Lexicon*, 302, 481.

xi   Strong, Strong's Dictionaries, e-Sword.

xii   Strong, *Strong's Dictionaries*, e-Sword.

xiii   Brown, Driver, and Briggs, *Lexicon*, 171.

xiv   Brown, Driver, and Briggs, *Lexicon*, 112.

xv   Strong, *Strong's Dictionaries*, e-Sword. Brown, Driver, and Briggs, *Lexicon*, 637.

xvi   Strong, *Strong's Dictionaries*, e-Sword. Brown, Driver, and Briggs, *Lexicon*, 101, 738.

xvii   Keil and Delitzsch, *Commentary,* 118. Clarke, *Commentary*, e-Sword. Albert Barnes, *Albert Barnes' Notes   on the Bible*, e-Sword.

xviii   Brown, Driver, and Briggs, *Lexicon*, 532.

xix   Brown, Driver, and Briggs, *Lexicon*, 933, 124.

xx   Strong, *Strong's Dictionaries*, e-Sword.

xxi   Strong, *Strong's Dictionaries*, e-Sword. Brown, Driver, and Briggs, *Lexicon*, 891.

xxii   Brown, Driver, and Briggs, *Lexicon*, e-Sword.

xxiii   Brown, Driver, and Briggs, *Lexicon*, 740.

xxiv   Strong, *Strong's Dictionaries*, e-Sword.

xxv   Clarke, *Commentary*, e-Sword.

xxvi   Brown, Driver, and Briggs, *Lexicon*, 138.

xxvii   Brown, Driver, and Briggs, *Lexicon*, 269.

CHAPTER SIX

i   Brown, Driver, and Briggs, *Lexicon*, 122. Strong, *Strong's Dictionaries*, e-Sword.

ii   Brown, Driver, and Briggs, *Lexicon*, 741, 796, 778.

iii   Strong, *Strong's Dictionaries*, e-Sword.

iv   Brown, Driver, and Briggs, *Lexicon*, 813, 738.

v   Barnes, *Notes on the Bible*, e-Sword.

vi   Brown, Driver, and Briggs, *Lexicon*, 804.

vii   Brown, Driver, and Briggs, *Lexicon*, 829.

viii   Brown, Driver, and Briggs, *Lexicon*, 678.

ix   Brown, Driver, and Briggs, *Lexicon*, 779.

x   Barnes, Notes on the Bible, e-Sword.

xi   Brown, Driver, and Briggs, *Lexicon*, e-Sword.

xii   Barnes, *Notes on the Bible,* e-Sword. Clarke, *Commentary*, e-Sword.

xiii   Strong, *Strong's Dictionaries*, e-Sword.

xiv   Strong, *Strong's Dictionaries*, e-Sword.

xv   Strong, *Strong's Dictionaries*, e-Sword.

xvi   Strong, *Strong's Dictionaries*, e-Sword. Brown, Driver, and Briggs, *Lexicon*, 1016.

xvii   Brown, Driver, and Briggs, *Lexicon*, 337.

xviii   Strong, *Strong's Dictionaries*, e-Sword.

xix   Brown, Driver, and Briggs, *Lexicon*, 337.

xx   Strong, *Strong's Dictionaries*, e-Sword.

xxi   Strong, Strong's Dictionaries, e-Sword. Brown, Driver, and Briggs, *Lexicon*, 575.
xxii   Brown, Driver, and Briggs, *Lexicon*, 864.
xxiii Brown, Driver, and Briggs, *Lexicon*, 824.

CHAPTER EIGHT

i   Barnes, Notes on the Bible, e-Sword.
ii   Jamieson, Fausset, and Brown, *Commentary*, e-Sword.
iii   Brown, Driver, and Briggs, *Lexicon*, e-Sword.
iv   Brown, Driver, and Briggs, *Lexicon*, e-Sword.
v   Jamieson, Fausset, Brown, *Commentary*, e-Sword.
vi   Brown, Driver, and Briggs, *Lexicon*, 195.
vii   Brown, Driver, and Briggs, *Lexicon*, 406.
viii   Keil and Delitzsch, *Commentary,* 138.